# PULSE *of the* RIVER

# PULSE *of* *the* RIVER

## Colorado Writers Speak for the Endangered Cache la Poudre

Edited by Gary Wockner and Laura Pritchett
Foreword by Rick Bass

*For the wild !*

ROCKY MOUNTAIN LAND LIBRARY

Johnson Books, Boulder

Published by Johnson Books, a Big Earth Publishing company,

3005 Center Green Drive, Suite 220, Boulder, Colorado 80301.

E-mail: books@bigearthpublishing.com

www.bigearthpublishing.com

1-800-258-5830

Cover design by Michael Cutter

Cover photo by Laura Katers

Text design and composition by Michael Cutter

9        8        7        6        5        4        3        2        1

Library of Congress Cataloging-in-Publication Data

Pulse of the river: Colorado writers speak for the endangered Cache la Poudre / edited by Gary Wockner and Laura Pritchett; foreword by Rick Bass.

        p.        cm.

    ISBN 1-55566-392-3

    1.  Natural history—Colorado—Cache la Poudre River. 2.  Human ecology—Colorado—Cache la Poudre River. 3.  Cache la Poudre River (Colo.)  I. Wockner, Gary. II. Pritchett, Laura, 1971-

    QH105.C6P85 2006

    508.788—dc22

                        2006025749

Printed in the United States of America

To all those who have loved this river,
those who do, and those who will.

To the river itself
in the hopes it will always run well and wild.

And to David Lauer, a true friend of the Poudre.
He will be missed.

# Contents

Foreword by Rick Bass. . . . . . . . . . . . . . . . . . . . . . . . . . . . . . . . ix

Introduction . . . . . . . . . . . . . . . . . . . . . . . . . . . . . . . . . . . . . . . xv

## Part 1: Maybe I'm in Love . . . . . . . . . . . . . . . . . . . . . . . . . 1

Jack Martin, "Narrows" . . . . . . . . . . . . . . . . . . . . . . . . . . . . . 3
Gary Wockner, "Against the Current" . . . . . . . . . . . . . . . . . . . 5
Tim Vaughan, "Haiku" . . . . . . . . . . . . . . . . . . . . . . . . . . . . . 16
Paul Miller, "Heart of the River" . . . . . . . . . . . . . . . . . . . . . 18
Evan Oakley, "Memoir" . . . . . . . . . . . . . . . . . . . . . . . . . . . . 27
Laura Pritchett, "Godzilla at the River" . . . . . . . . . . . . . . . . 29
Clarissa Pinkola Estés, "The Soul Is a River, The River
   Has a Soul" . . . . . . . . . . . . . . . . . . . . . . . . . . . . . . . . . . . 41
Todd Simmons, "Death and Decay in the Poudre" . . . . . . . . . . 49

## Part 2: A Kind of Vertigo . . . . . . . . . . . . . . . . . . . . . . . . . 55

John Calderazzo, "Herons" . . . . . . . . . . . . . . . . . . . . . . . . . . 57
J. D. Phillips, "Rejecting Fast-Food Fishing:
   Angling the Upper Cache la Poudre" . . . . . . . . . . . . . . . . . 59
Robert King, "Poudre Poems" . . . . . . . . . . . . . . . . . . . . . . . . 64
Deborah Dimon, "The Decomposition of Bone Woman" . . . . . . 67
Steve Miles, "First Night Without Rain" . . . . . . . . . . . . . . . . 78
Cynthia Melcher, "Desperate for River Refugia" . . . . . . . . . . . 80
Veronica Patterson, "Following the River" . . . . . . . . . . . . . . . 90
Ruth Obee, "Whitewater Rafting on the Poudre During a
   Mountain Storm" . . . . . . . . . . . . . . . . . . . . . . . . . . . . . . . 92

## Part 3: Spiral of Our Life . . . . . . . . . . . . . . . . . . . . . . . . . 95

Christopher Mulrooney, "Pass" . . . . . . . . . . . . . . . . . . . . . . . 97
Mark Easter, "The Lady's Last Dance" . . . . . . . . . . . . . . . . . 98
Patricia Nolan, "Five Haiku for Cache la Poudre River" . . . . . 112
Ellen Wohl, "Pulse of the River" . . . . . . . . . . . . . . . . . . . . . 114
Ted Lardner, "Poudre River Poem" . . . . . . . . . . . . . . . . . . . 124

Diane Fromme, "The Mirror in the River" . . . . . . . . . . . . . . . . 125
Carl R. Nassar, "Under the Benevolent Influence of a
 Water Deity" . . . . . . . . . . . . . . . . . . . . . . . . . . . . . . . . . . . . . . . . . 134
John Calderazzo, "Highway Flagman" . . . . . . . . . . . . . . . . . . . 141
David Rozgonyi, "The Postcard" . . . . . . . . . . . . . . . . . . . . . . . . 143

## Part 4: Our Bodies Are Rivers . . . . . . . . . . . . . . . . . . . . . 153

Steve Miles, "Kingfisher" . . . . . . . . . . . . . . . . . . . . . . . . . . . . . 154
Todd Mitchell, "Surfing the River" . . . . . . . . . . . . . . . . . . . . . 156
Scott Woods, "Sudden Swim (with apologies to
 Robert Service)" . . . . . . . . . . . . . . . . . . . . . . . . . . . . . . . . . . . . 162
Ian Ellis, "A Subtle Doubt" . . . . . . . . . . . . . . . . . . . . . . . . . . . 164
Blair Oliver, "Stations" . . . . . . . . . . . . . . . . . . . . . . . . . . . . . . . 165
Lary Kleeman, "Watercolor" . . . . . . . . . . . . . . . . . . . . . . . . . . 174
Kathleen Dean, "Ashes" . . . . . . . . . . . . . . . . . . . . . . . . . . . . . . 176
Evan Oakley, "Maenad" . . . . . . . . . . . . . . . . . . . . . . . . . . . . . . 179
Kerri Mitchell, "Coming Back" . . . . . . . . . . . . . . . . . . . . . . . . 181
Jack Martin, "Snapping Turtle" . . . . . . . . . . . . . . . . . . . . . . . . 186
Bill Tremblay, "On the Trail of the Sublime Along
 the Poudre" . . . . . . . . . . . . . . . . . . . . . . . . . . . . . . . . . . . . . . . . . 187
James Galvin, "Cache la Poudre" . . . . . . . . . . . . . . . . . . . . . . 195

Appendix: Organizations Working to Preserve the
 Cache la Poudre River . . . . . . . . . . . . . . . . . . . . . . . . . . . . . . 197

# Foreword
## Rick Bass

Sometimes things have to get real bad before they get better. When a river goes away—goes underground, disappearing entirely—well, I would say that definitely would qualify as a wake-up call, a hint that things are maybe not so rosy. I suppose the only thing worse than a river going underground, as the Cache la Poudre has begun to do in places, would be for it to die entirely, and for even that underground water to be used up, mined and gone away forever, extinct, like the unraveled strands of DNA whose mysterious twinings once described the shape and being of some fantastic species.

One of the things that impress me about this collective group of Poudre activists is the unabashed acknowledgment of the spiritual value the Cache la Poudre River provides to the lives of the contributors—this river has healed and restored their sometimes-injured lives. There is nothing abstract or hypothetical about these testimonies: This is real-time restoration, on a scale that Blue Cross/Blue Shield might appreciate, and done absolutely on the cheap. Of course it makes sense, from a perspective of moral reciprocity, for those healed and restored by the river's presence to be compelled now to return the favor; and hence this book, this testimony, this commitment to a vision.

Why does the Cache la Poudre matter? A silly question, if one describes the river only in terms of water, for everyone knows that water is the second-most important element critical to our minute-by-minute survival, much less to the endurance of civilizations, and the expansion of culture. But one of the things I find valuable about this collection is the other perspectives and references attached to the definition of this river, where it is no longer treated as a mere impoundment for a fairly static and measurable quantity of a chemical compound but is instead finally afforded the dignity and import of a living process. In this collection, the river is tributary of scientific inquiry, as well as nurturer of other life processes; the river is a source of artistic inspiration, the river is therapy, the river is the foundation of culture, and it is the basis of economic sustenance.

This last element is one I ponder at length. In any environmental struggle these days, you can count on environmentalists to increasingly roll out the gold-plated economic models that show a wild river is worth a lot of money—not value, that sometimes abstract and arguable concept—but cold hard cash, as easily enumerated as the days of one's mortal life. But so strange is our society these days that I think we have learned how to incorporate money—money, if not wealth—into any transaction whatsoever. I suspect we could find an equation wherein an intact mountain might "make" us a million dollars, and I suppose we could find an equation where that same mountain, disassembled, might also make a million.

And while the artistic side of me sometimes feels a bit funny about embracing economics in the effort to save a thing of beauty, it would be irresponsible to gloss over or avoid the fact that keeping the Poudre alive makes good business sense. As with any business decision, there remain hidden and unaccounted costs and variables. The solution, therefore, will require tempering, creativity, work; of which this book, and this collective voice, is but one small and vital beginning, partly symbolic but also partly functional, for I know that these voices speak for many more than the authors themselves.

Again, the irony—or, to some aesthetes like myself, the almost distasteful reality—is that this reciprocity between river and riverkeepers isn't just good for your soul and your health and the land, but also the local economy. Maybe one day soon there will be a generation to whom such realizations come not as a surprise but are instead understood as if instinctively to be true. I have labored all my life within the old cultural paradigm—a brainwashing, really—that says what's good for the land must therefore be bad for people's jobs. As such, the feeling of wonder and even stupefaction that attends to my reading of one study after another in which this is not at all the case must be somewhat like the sensation a long-time prisoner, unfairly incarcerated in the first place, experiences on the day when the gates finally swing open. And the metaphor is apt, for it is thick steel gates that will hold the Poudre back.

———

It's a daunting, sensitive, and tender thing to see people who love a landscape—in this case, the living thread of an injured and dying river—putting aside, to paraphrase the poet Mary Oliver, their "one and precious life" to take up the defense of something voiceless. I'm familiar with this image, this response, as an activist as well as a wanderer out on the land. In the Yaak Valley of extreme northwest Montana—the Land the Wilderness Act Forgot, where there is still not a single acre of designated wilderness, despite it being one of the wildest and most biologically diverse million-acre landmasses in the Lower 48—the part of the landscape that has been left wild and roadless is still capable of not just amazing and astounding a visitor or resident, but healing.

Our little grassroots group, the Yaak Valley Forest Council—much like these friends of the Cache la Poudre—has set about the reclamation of an injured landscape, combining that restoration with other stewardship projects, metamorphosing a negative back into a positive, and coincidentally, bringing in millions of dollars of jobs, over only a very few years. This is neither the stuff of alchemy, nor of creation, but it is certainly the fabric of good manners, and of moral responsibility: And again, by such actions, who can say who is helped the most, the river or the human?

Words are cheap, veteran environmental activists such as Ed Abbey and Doug Peacock have said; one bold act is worth a thousand books, to which I might add a suggested postscript: Sometimes the mild or moderate or enduring actions are worth the most of all. Dream big, dream bold, but in that vast wasteland across which one must travel to reach the further shore of that dream, there are endless meetings, endless occasions on which the heart's wild longings, tempers, and desires must be restrained, endless alliances, endless dead-end opportunities or ideas, wasted phone calls. Some fun.

I imagine further that most of the participants in this volume, as they continue with their hearts' labors, and as their hearts—as do those of all activists—desiccate, they will go back to the river yet again for renewal and steadying.

———

In reading these accounts, these testimonies, I'm buoyed also by the revelations of science, which can be a great source of strength when faith grows faint or weak or weary. Sure, I love the Poudre with all my heart, and I know it to be a magical place beyond our measurements or understanding, but look at this: Microinvertebrate diversity as a function of ecosystem health increases exponentially in an integrated flow regime between $x$ and $y$ cubic feet per second during the spring, summer, and fall, when mean low temperatures do not fall below z degrees Fahrenheit.

The ability to perceive, like a shadow, the hidden rhythms and patterns that used to underlie a certain natural process, and which might still underlie it, is nothing less than the ability to understand the existence of something even in its absence. This is perhaps a definition of faith, but perhaps it is also one of the greatest demonstrations of human, or animal, intelligence.

In this book, geologist Ellen Wohl speaks of a "seed shadow," wherein dams alter and even block the distribution of seeds that would otherwise have been carried downstream and disseminated bankside. Over time, those species then die out downstream, vanishing, individual by individual, cut off from the main source of their earlier distribution as well as sustenance: And, like revisionist history or anti-history, the dams begin slowly to un-write the patterns of downstream vegetation. "The outstanding scientific discovery of the twentieth century," wrote American ecologist Aldo Leopold,

> is ... the complexity of the land organism. Only those who know the most about it can appreciate how little we know about it. The last word in ignorance is the man who says of an animal or plant: "What good is it?" If the land mechanism as a whole is good, then every part is good, whether we understand it or not. If the biota, in the course of aeons, has built something we like but do not understand, then who but a fool would discard seemingly useless parts? To keep every cog and wheel is the first precaution of intelligent tinkering.

Again, these are lessons not just in biology, but in morality. What are all the costs of an action? Too often, we are not properly acknowledging either our costs or our benefits.

A person could spend a lifetime studying such stories, and such lessons. There is nothing about the river that is not a useful and powerful *metaphor*; and there is nothing, still, about the river that is not also useful and powerful *reality*.

The Cache la Poudre is not yet an absent shadow, dim memory, buried beneath a giant (if doomed and temporary) toxic slackwater bathtub; nor has it yet gone all the way underground, leaving nothing more than a traced depression in the dust and cobble of where-it-once-lived. An imaginary dam exists between the way many used to look at rivers and the way many are now beginning to perceive them. The future lies downstream, and the authors of this volume seem to me to be like engineers, removing certain old and faulty designs and participating in something that is nothing less than a resurrection of an older world, a world better made and fitted, and so sophisticated and elegant, that we barely know what to do with it, other than first loving it.

And from that instinctive response of knowledge and healing—for all the participants, human and nonhuman—the river, and the civilization that has grown up perched at its edges, will resume and continue, stronger than ever for having been tested.

# Introduction
## Gary Wockner and Laura Pritchett

The river was dry, and we mean *bone dry*. Okay, sure, there were a few skanky pools dotting the low spots in the path of rocks stretching to the east and the west. We walked right down the middle of what used to be the river, hopping on stones, small and big. We hadn't intended to pick this day—this totally *dead* river day—for our hike. Our goal was to discuss the idea for creating a "Poudre River Anthology," a collection of new writing from local writers and poets that celebrated the threatened Cache la Poudre. Were we too late?

It was early spring 2005, and we were walking along the Poudre as it runs by the small ranch where Laura grew up, just northwest of Fort Collins, in the town of LaPorte. About a hundred yards farther upstream, we saw Laura's dad and one of her brothers. They were out fixing irrigation pipe, mucking around in the mud beside a drippy and rusted section of 10-inch pipe, trying to splice the problem area with a coffee can. We hopped to the side of the river and over a dam-and-diversion structure, and then we visited with Laura's dad for a few minutes. After Laura described the reason for our outing, he looked over at the river and softly said, "Yeah, I've sure never seen it this low, not in thirty years."

We continued our hike up the first foothill on the west end of the ranch, and we discussed our plans for the anthology. The dead river left kind of an eerie feeling in our guts, and our discussion thereafter had a weird and hopeless quality to it. It was, however, a beautiful Rocky Mountain day—the sun was shining brightly, and the view from the hill above Laura's family ranch offered an optimistic vision—and so we laid out our plan and set a timeline.

To be honest, we know that hope does exist for the Poudre, just as hope exists for all Western rivers. On the very day of our hike, the river was flowing strongly just four miles upstream at the mouth of Poudre Canyon. Near Laura's ranch, however, the water had all been sucked out and diverted before it got there.

Although the mainstem of the Poudre is the last undammed river along the Front Range of Colorado, the Poudre is still one of the most managed and plumbed of Colorado's rivers. A person or city or company owns the right to every drop of Poudre water, and when and where that water goes is regulated by hundreds of millions of dollars of diversion structures and ditches, and many more millions of dollars of water lawyers, administrators, and policy analysts. There is water, to be sure; it just doesn't usually flow down the actual river bed.

Further, as if the Poudre wasn't diminished enough, its future is in even more jeopardy. As of this writing, three large dam-and-reservoir projects are in the works that will take ever more of the Poudre's flow and divert it out of the main channel toward the unquenchable thirst of its users. In Larimer County, more water projects are planned than in anywhere in the Western United States. During our hike we were standing at "ground zero" for the next generation of dam-building and Western water fights. One of these projects—the Glade Reservoir—is a massive monolith that will cost over $300 million and take so much peak flow out of the Poudre that it will turn the downstream river through Fort Collins and out to Greeley into a semi-dry ditch.

And that's not right.

As we sat atop the hill overlooking Laura's ranch, we refused to be depressed, and instead gave ourselves a challenge: Unlike the water users who seek the Poudre's demise, our goal was to celebrate not the water, but the actual *river*. We hoped to reach out to the public and decisionmakers with a new and different voice—one that loves rivers. We firmly believe there is hope for the Cache la Poudre and all Western rivers. We firmly believe the Poudre can run strongly again, not only in the canyon west of Fort Collins, but also below the mouth of the canyon and all the way out to Greeley. We firmly believe that with the right message, the right stories, and the right leadership, the Poudre can be newly appreciated.

We believe in the Poudre's rebirth.

———

Writers and poets are an independent bunch. When you ask a writer or poet to speak—and especially when you ask them to speak and don't pay them—what you get is their core, their truth. They have nothing to gain but their stock-in-trade: their honesty, integrity, and masterful gifts of storytelling.

So when we asked all the writers and poets in northern Colorado to speak for the Poudre, we had no idea what they would send us. But we knew it wouldn't be what we usually read in the newspaper about the Poudre—some kind of soulless chamber-of-commerce spin in which the proud masters of nature harness the wild Poudre for the collective good of humankind and everybody lives happily ever after.

Instead, these writers sent us unique and provocative essays and poems that speak to the heart and soul of the Cache la Poudre. And the more we read and edited these stories, the more that heart and soul came through. Collectively, these writers and poets seem to be saying that our society does a wonderful job of filling our pocketbooks, of feeding our stomachs, of utilizing nature for human purposes, of filling our brains with information. Yes, we do that well. But, these writers also say, in doing all those other things, our hearts and souls can remain empty.

To fill those empty spots—to fill our hearts and souls—a new story of Western rivers must be told, one that focuses on sustainability and on living with a closer connection to the land and water. One in which the Cache la Poudre River—which is, after all, the reason why this whole part of northern Colorado was settled in the first place—plays a larger physical and spiritual role in our lives.

After we sent out our call for papers, the stories and poems poured in just like the Poudre's waters pour down the canyon. We set about organizing these stories into common themes. Four categories emerged.

The first part, "Maybe I'm in Love," focuses on the healing power of the Poudre. Several writers have experienced some sort of dis-ease in their lives and have used the Poudre to help heal that schism. They've waded in the Poudre, ran around it, stood beside it, watched it. The Poudre's moving water, and the reconnection with nature along the waterway, helped heal body and mind.

The second part, "A Kind of Vertigo," deals with appreciating and learning about the Poudre and its environs. Writers and poets found birds, bones, fish, and even human inhabitants that fascinated and enthralled. In this section, writers celebrate the natural gifts of the Poudre and help readers see these gifts through a trained storyteller's eye.

The third part, "Spiral of Our Life," covers the Poudre over longer lengths of time. One writer, Mark Easter, unearthed some original sketches drawn in 1869 during the first geological survey of the area; and then he and another contributor, Tim Vaughan, photographed these same places in 2005. The comparisons are startling. Other writers focus on the river over their own life spans and discuss how repeatedly visiting the Poudre over the years has helped them see the changes in their own lives as well as appreciate the constant drum of natural life.

Finally, the last part is titled "Our Bodies Are Rivers." The Poudre, it turns out, tests us and teaches us. Through the Poudre—wading in it, watching it, kayaking it—we learn about ourselves. We go to the Poudre to be challenged, to feel, to grow as individuals.

As you read through the book, we're sure you may see overlap in these sections. We invite you to think about other connections and categories as well—after all, that is what rivers do best, invite us to see new angles, to think about new ideas, or to examine old ideas from a different perspective.

Overall, the writers and poets in this book have expressed a strong kinship metaphor—they seem to be saying that our bodies, our lives, and our beings are much like rivers. In a literal sense, it's so easy to see how our kinship to rivers could have emerged. We pour water in the top of our bodies and it flows right back out the bottom. Scientists tell us that our bodies are made up of two-thirds water, and the flow of liquids and blood through our bodies is certainly river-like. Even more, when someone's blood stops flowing, that person dies, as does the river die with the stopping of water.

We invite you to try this: Take this book down to the Poudre River, or your local river wherever you live. Find a nice spot where the sun is sprinkling through the cottonwoods and you can hear the river dappling over rocks. Lie down on your back and prop your head up on a log or bush. Point your head upstream and point your feet downstream so that the river is flowing by you, head-to-toe, and then start reading the pages. We wonder if what happened to all the contributors will happen to you too: The river first seems to flow by you, and then it seems to flow through you. It gets in your blood. The stories and poems in this book might do the same.

While you're turning pages and immersing yourself in the Poudre, please know too that we're not just writers and poets, we are not just analyzers of the human condition, or chroniclers of ecological and spiritual decay. We are much more: We are advocates.

As we said: The river was dry, and we mean *bone* dry. And that's not right.

To help restore the Poudre, we are donating all the royalties from the publication of this book to the Colorado Water Trust, an extraordinary new organization dedicated to "acquiring, or assisting others in acquiring water rights or interests in water rights, using voluntary approaches from willing owners, for conservation benefits" (www.coloradowatertrust.org). It is our opinion that the Colorado Water Trust is the best organization in the state working with the best people and setting the most realistic goals for the future of sustainable Colorado rivers, including our beloved Cache la Poudre.

So, please enjoy the dancing sun, the rippling water, and the words herein. And when you need a break, walk down and stick your feet in the river. Feel the water curve around your toes, watch it make little eddies around your ankles. Know that it's not too late, if we try, if we care, to save the Poudre.

# PART 1

# Maybe I'm in Love

Humans have a special kinship with rivers. Prior to advanced civilization, nearly all our activities took place within a stone's throw of water. The writers in this section strongly suggest that this kinship goes a full step farther—toward healing. Whether the cause be the inhuman mechanistic society around us or the unknown watery machine inside of us, the writers and poets here have experienced some kind of dis-ease, and then turned to the Cache la Poudre's waters for healing. With the potential demise of the Poudre, contributor Gary Wockner suggests that "we are trying to kill what has drawn us here, what sustains us, and what heals us."

# Narrows

## Jack Martin

*Jack Martin was a professional river guide for fifteen years, and he has rafted many of the rivers in the Rocky Mountain West.  His poems have appeared in* Ploughshares, Black Warrior Review, The Journal, *and other magazines. In "Narrows"—titled for a section of the Poudre with the same name—he speaks to the great life of the river, and how it reflects itself in our hearts.*

Here, the water says her name.
White chance castles
in the constriction,
walls of error and happiness.
The right kiss works
this same way.
Something French
happens to the heart.
Call it poudre or life,
green-bellied creatures
finning in the pools, terror
at the surface
where the body meets
the air. The soul
has gradient and volume.
Spring is an error
that cannot be righted.
Autumn and winter
are equally sad,
crazy with beauty and rocks.
The water falls
into gray smoke.
All of this longing

in one place. Maybe
I'm bleeding.
Maybe I'm in love.
In eddies
our thoughts cling together
for as long as they can.
I should have been more faithful.
The current is without doubt.
At the bottom of these centuries,
drowned in rock,
her name is a sob that lasts.
Extend a hand.

# Against the Current
## Gary Wockner

*Gary Wockner, a creative writer and ecologist, lives in Fort Collins just a few blocks from the Poudre River. Gary grew up beside a slow-moving muddy river in central Illinois. Most recently, he coedited and contributed to* Comeback Wolves: Western Writers Welcome the Wolf Home. *In his essay, "Against the Current," Gary draws from his life roles as parent, activist, and ecologist, and discusses some of the formal issues surrounding the conservation of the Poudre, and how living near the Poudre has helped galvanize his passion for saving it.*

The water swirls around her legs and makes little eddies as she walks upstream. I can tell she feels the drag against the current, as if each leg weighs fifty pounds. She leans forward. I love to watch her lean. "Lean," I think to myself. "Move that water. Go where you want." I don't say it out loud, but that's what I'm thinking, what I'm trying to say, though in different words.

I'm in the Cache la Poudre River wading with my eight-year-old daughter, Julia. It's late spring, a Tuesday afternoon, and although flowing tumultuously up in Poudre Canyon to the west, the river in town is still nearly dry, its flow diverted by dams, dikes, and ditches before it reaches us. But right here in this one spot just below a little riffle as the river runs nearby our house, the water comes up to Julia's knees and is moving quickly enough to make eddies on the backs of our legs.

I could be at work, but I'm not. Instead, we're looking for craw-dads, Julia and I, and we've found dozens. They hide and dart throughout the small rounded rocks on the river bottom. Julia's got a stick and she's poking them out, and then we examine how quickly they swim through the water as they flap their tails backward. They dart around, always backward, claws facing forward, defensive.

We find all sorts of other critters too. Julia points out caddisfly eggs stuck on the sides and bottoms of several rocks. She's been down here with her school class, and they've studied the river and much of its flora and fauna. Small minnows circle our legs, and one small trout swims in a pool just ten feet downstream. On the banks we see many small trees ringed with beaver cuttings, and we see a few willow trees completely chewed down, their pointed stumps and tendrils circled with the chopping pattern of beaver teeth.

Julia pokes and prods at the crawdads as we wade around. "Dad," she says, her face glowing, "Look!" And I do. Or at least I try to. But you know how it is when you're a parent—my mind is in fifty different places, and I'm thinking about work, about making dinner, about fixing the porch roof, about the Poudre's politics and activism I'm involved in, and about what the hell to do with my life. But I try to fit in these river escapades with my family because I love the river. I love the way the river makes us all feel.

"Dad," Julia exclaims, pointing, "that one's got a huge pincher arm!" Wow. Indeed it does—it's an inch long, and the crawdad is waving its arm at us like we're perilous predators hell-bent on murder and destruction. Our intentions are more benevolent today, but I wish I did not feel that, at a broader level, the crawdad is right. If it knew what de-watered future could be in store for its habitat, it might then wave that pincher even more aggressively.

As we wade in the river, Julia asks me dozens of questions of a biological sort, and I know only a few answers. I enjoy rivers, but I don't study their ecology. Mostly, I just love coming here. Three or four times a week, I have a jogging route that leaves our house, which is a few blocks away, and takes me on a two-mile loop around the river. On some weekdays like today, and on weekends, our family comes down here together.

When we moved to Fort Collins several years back, I looked for a house as close to the Poudre as possible. The Poudre flows through town amidst a broad swath of natural areas encompassing thousands of acres and numerous ponds. It is beautiful, and though far from pristine, it offers a natural respite—an escape—from the ever-growing metropolitan area of northern Colorado.

Over the past few years, our family has walked the Poudre's banks, biked and ran along the paved path that runs miles beside it, waded in it, swam in it, chased crawdads in it, and watched wildlife around it. I come down here almost every day for a walk, a run, or some kind of adventure with the kids. I've developed a strong attachment to this river, even a kind of defensiveness. The Poudre's greenness pulls me to it—I don't understand this, I just know that it is true, and always has been. I was raised beside a river, and ever since then I have been pulled to the greenness of rivers, often against the current. Today, Julia and I lean forward, into it.

————

The Cache la Poudre is an extremely threatened river. With its headwaters at the north, west, and southern edges of Larimer County amidst three mountainous forks, the river enjoys relative freedom at its pristine mountain beginnings. But as these forks converge dozens of miles downstream near the mouth of Poudre Canyon, the threats grow immensely. Currently, three new dam-and-reservoir projects are in planning stages near the confluence of the Poudre's forks. In total, these projects will cost nearly a half-billion dollars of taxpayer money.

The reasons for the Poudre's imminent demise are the usual: ever-growing populations of people (including me and my family) along the northern Front Range of Colorado and increasing demands by rural agriculture. These are, in fact, the very same perpetrators that currently use almost all of the Poudre's water and have Julia and me standing in an almost-dry river on this late-spring day. As the Poudre flows out of the canyon and onto the plains through Fort Collins, about 90 percent of its water is already sucked out in a massive network of over two dozen ditches, dikes, and dams.

Here near my house, which is three miles downstream from the mouth of the canyon, the river is nearly dry about eight months a year. Thirty flat miles farther downstream, where the Poudre meets the South Platte River southeast of Greeley, the Poudre is a mere whisper of its former self—its once majestic and sparklingly clear flow has been transformed into a fifteen-foot-wide muddy and stinking ditch.

This story would have a nice good-versus-evil spin to it—the usual bit of illegal human greed versus natural ecological health—if it weren't for one major factor: The law runs against the river. Water in Colorado, and throughout much of the West, is legally a commodity—not a public resource like forests, open space, and wildlife—and every drop of water is more-or-less owned by some entity that has a full legal right to use it. This idea, called "beneficial use," stipulates that water must be used primarily for human financial benefit. And further, if you own that water right and let it flow by in the river without using it for your financial benefit, you can lose your water right and someone else can legally take it.

The main impetus for these laws began back in the early days of the West's colonization when water was used in gold and silver mining operations. At that time, few demands were made on water for agriculture, and Colorado's population was minimal. Further, nobody was thinking about ecological devastation to rivers, and further yet, very few people were using Colorado water for human enjoyment. The law thus stipulated that water rights should be owned and used, and so every drop of the tens-of-millions-of-acre-feet of water that flows off Colorado's spectacular snowcapped mountains is a legal commodity much like a crop of corn or hillside deposit of silver ore. The right to use Colorado's water is, in fact, bought and sold on open markets somewhat like corn and silver.

Times have changed drastically, but the law has only changed a smidgen. The West's culture, as a whole, is grappling with a new watery vision, one that sees profound uses in functioning ecological river systems and finds incredible enjoyment in rivers. We increasingly recognize that the river itself and the myriad species and ecological processes around the river serve intrinsic and necessary purposes. We also paddle rivers, build bike paths beside them, fish them, wade them, watch them, photograph them, and write by them. But the law still stipulates for the primacy of human financial "beneficial uses," and the entities that are planning the current dams and diversions on the Poudre—and they include cities, ditch companies, and farmers—still own the water rights and have every legal option to develop and use the river.

This kind of schism—where laws and entrenched financial systems lag behind ideas and visions—is at the heart of the West's water chaos. This schism underlies both of the biggest uses of Poudre water—irrigated agriculture and residential use—and thus the future health of the Poudre remains murky at best.

About 80 percent of the Poudre's water is used to grow irrigated agricultural crops in Larimer County and on the eastern Colorado plains. Even though irrigated agricultural is an ecological misfit in the West, it has a long history of water rights ownership dating back to just after the mining era, and it has very important political clout through Colorado and the West. A smaller amount of the Poudre's water—roughly 10 percent—is used in residential homes and to grow water-guzzling bluegrass lawns along the northern Front Range. A green and manicured lawn is a potent symbol of middle-class success, and even though lawns are also profound ecological misfits in the West's dry environments, most homeowners still choose lawns for landscaping.

These two main uses of the Poudre's water offer significant challenges to any effort to restore the river's health. Additionally, future demand on water continues to increase due to expected population growth. Conspiring in this future growth, the various chambers of commerce and economic development commissions of northern Colorado are spending millions of dollars every year luring more people and businesses to the area.

While these threats continue to grow, it is equally true that a mixture of hope, activism, and technology to save the Poudre is also growing. In the context of irrigated agriculture, many new irrigation technologies exist that could save one-third to one-half of the water that is currently used in crop production. Additionally, newly developed farming methods like crop rotations and dryland crop species could also save water. The recent Western drought has forced many farmers to consider new irrigation and farming methods and has forced government leaders to begin developing incentives and policies that will allow agricultural producers to sustain their farms with less irrigation water.

Residential water use could also be curtailed without the loss of the public's amenities. Drought-resistant landscaping is increasingly available, and myriad low-water residential irrigation technologies are on the market. Additionally, indoor water use could be curtailed with various low-water appliances. As more people speak out against water waste, some leaders of northern Colorado cities are beginning to embrace these new landscape aesthetics and technologies and the government policies and incentive programs that reward water conservation.

The word "reward" is likely the key ingredient that will help save the Poudre, because the three dam-and-diversion projects in the works have yet to be scrutinized from an economic standpoint. Money can be spent one of two ways in these water issues: (1) to develop more storage through dams and reservoirs, or (2) through water conservation rewards and programs. During the latest drought, for example, the City of Fort Collins spent only $200,000 on a marketing campaign promoting residential water conservation, and the public responded by cutting water use by 10 percent. That 10 percent amounted to 3,000 acre-feet of water, and at the time of the drought, one acre-foot of water was selling for $17,000. Thus, the public saved $51,000,000 worth of water by spending $200,000 on a marketing campaign. Myriad rewards and government policies that promote agricultural and residential water conservation could have similar effects. Water can be conserved much more cheaply than it can be impounded behind dams and without any of a dam's ecological costs.

Conserving water, though, will only get us halfway toward a healthier Poudre. Because current water law requires "beneficial use" that forces water owners to "use or lose" the water to another downstream user, those laws will have to be changed before any of that conserved water remains in the river. Fortunately, Colorado is beginning to address this underlying problem. Forward-thinking legal efforts are in the works that will allow the transfer of ownership of water back to rivers for their ecological health and for human enjoyment. Currently, in several counties around the state, small amounts of water have been transferred back to rivers for fishing, whitewater rafting, and kayaking.

After we have the legal mechanisms in place, what is also needed, and is just beginning to occur, is the creation of financial mechanisms to buy the rights to water from willing sellers and transfer those rights back to rivers. Just as we have "open space funds," there's no reason why we can't have "river health funds" that buy rights to water at market prices and keep water in the river for the greater good. Already, some forward-thinking individuals, organizations, and cities in Colorado have donated water for instream flow rights in their local rivers, and are considering buying rights to water for whitewater parks and other ecological benefits.

In short, the Cache la Poudre River does not have to die. Many folks are working hard to heal our water schism, and here in northern Colorado along the Cache la Poudre, we sit at an opportunistic forefront of vision and hope. The Poudre is extremely threatened, but ironically, it may be that very threat—that necessity-as-the-mother-of-invention—that pushes us toward a more healthy river, and healthy life.

———

I have a confession to make: I am extremely biased toward this river. As Julia and I wade in the river and poke at crawdads, I watch a few joggers run by on the dirt paths that surround the river, and this scene reminds me of my own jogging regimen and the reason for my bias.

I went through a "period," you might call it, that lasted ten years where I didn't exercise at all. It was a rough ten years—I was starting a family, launching a career, and we moved around the country too many times. During that period, I felt like each leg weighed a hundred pounds, like I was continually walking against the current. The sun didn't seem to shine, my vision was cloudy, and my body and mind were ever more molded around an office chair in a fluorescent-lit room. When I wasn't sitting in an office chair, it seemed I was either shoveling goopy baby food into my daughters' mouths, or shoveling clothes into the washing machine. In the worst moments, it felt like my skin was crawling off my body, and like the neurons in my head were coated with a thick mold.

And so when we moved to Fort Collins and started looking for a more permanent place to live, I was determined to begin anew and find a place to heal my schism. I got out the maps of town and looked for all the green spots, and then I drove and walked around the town's many natural areas. The Poudre's greenness jumped out at me as it coursed through the northern part of the city. We ended up buying a small, cheap house that was five minutes away from work, schools, and downtown, and two blocks from the river.

I was determined and inspired, and my healing process began. I started walking along the river for a few months, and then later I tried running. Unfortunately though, my hundred-pound legs continued to linger; my other responsibilities continued to sap too much time and energy. A few months later I tried again, then stopped. And then a few months after that I tried again, and then stopped again. My off-and-on attempts at exercise and healing went on for one year, and then two, and then three. I made very little progress.

And then I remembered what they said, the psychologists and therapists, about the airplane's oxygen mask. They use this metaphor of the airplane losing cabin pressure, and all the oxygen masks falling down from the overhead compartment. They tell you to picture yourself sitting amidst your family on the plane. You are beginning to suffocate; your children are beginning to suffocate. You are faced with a dilemma. Your children are too small to grab the masks, and so you have to decide whether to help your children put on their masks or to put on your mask first. Should you save your children or attempt to save yourself?

And here is their answer: In order to save your children, you must put on your own mask first. You must first breathe the fresh oxygen, regain your vision and your strength, and then help your children put on their masks. You can't do anything worthwhile for yourself or your family while your own health suffers. In order to save others, you must first save yourself.

In the fourth year of my healing process, I began anew, though differently. I saved up some money, and then I stepped back from my career and began working halftime in a lower-responsibility position. And then I started running again. After a few months around my little loop here along the Poudre, my body started looking like its old self. Muscles again appeared, my breathing became stronger, and my legs returned to lightness. Two months later, I could run farther than my loop, or I could do the loop everyday.

A few more months of running around the Poudre and another unexpected change occurred: The sun came out; enthusiasm and optimism returned. Opportunity again knocked, and within another few months I found myself working harder and longer again, but now on new issues of personal passion.

And so I am biased toward this river. I have a personal connection to the water around my loop. The more water that's in the river, the better I feel. The less water in the river, the angrier I get and the more

I vow to defend and restore the Poudre. I love this river, but it's not a humble soft love. It's a manic running love. It's an angry love. It's a fighting love. It's also an educated and politically astute love. It looks toward long-term vision, and like all good love everywhere, it is relentless.

And I am not the only one. In the seven years I have lived near the Poudre, I have noticed something else: The city, county, and state have spent millions of dollars extending the paved path that runs beside the river, and have also spent millions buying and developing the natural areas around the river. The path now runs over ten miles from almost the mouth of Poudre Canyon all the way out east to I-25 amidst tens-of-thousands of acres of public open space, and this path and open space is used by tens-of-thousands of people every month. Plans are in the works to extend the path all the way to Greeley.

Further, since I've started walking and running this loop, the unofficial dirt paths along the Poudre have widened considerably. Six years ago, these paths used to be just a foot wide, or sometimes they were mere bent-down grassy strips running through the brush. But now, most of the running paths along the Poudre are two-feet wide or more, are beat down to solid dirt, and are etched with runners' shoeprints. Not a run goes by where I don't meet other runners—sometimes a few dozen runners—along the Poudre's banks.

There is a critical irony in all of this: We are planning to dam and drain the Poudre at the very same time we are spending millions of dollars to preserve and enhance the natural areas around it. We are trying to kill what has drawn us here, what sustains us, and what heals us.

And so I will put it this way: The Poudre has many friends, and we are not humble, soft people. We are biased, we are defenders and fighters who enjoy running against the current, and we are growing stronger with each lap along the Poudre's willowy banks.

————

As Julia and I continue to look for crawdads, a small willow branch floats nearby. One of its ends is pointed like a spear with precise chew marks circling the point. The branch has been chiseled off by one of the many beavers that inhabit the river and nearby ponds. Julia grabs the branch and we examine the chew marks—they are mesmerizing in their uniformity and depth, and I marvel at the skill and relentlessness required of that job.

"I wanna take this home," Julia says.

"Uh-huh," I say back. Our house is already littered with Julia's river treasures—sticks, rocks, squirrel skeletons, dead crawdads, birds' nests, and all sorts of swamp-things like pond scum and cattails. Julia is one of those kids who brings everything home. Every few months, the stink in her bedroom gets so bad that I have to clean it out and move all of her reeking decaying river treasures outside.

We throw the stick up on the bank for saving and return our attention to the river bottom. With the sun shining brightly overhead, the river rocks shine back at us like jewels. It's hard to believe they are the same grayish rocks that line the shore. But the water works wonders; its wetness illuminates like fingernail polish. Julia first learned this a few years back—she'd gather these beautiful wet rocks, but by the time we got home, the rocks had dried and turned a grayish dull hue. Not long after that, she discovered rock polishers, and then a polisher eventually turned in our greenhouse, its 24/7 whirring noise softly piercing the air. And then eventually the small polished rocks covered all the surfaces in our house.

As an hour goes by, Julia and I turn over rocks, inspect crawdads, chase minnows, pick up beaver cuttings, and watch a great blue heron and a red-winged blackbird fly by. A huge mass of turkey vultures circles overhead. The wind lightly flows down the river, and we can catch just a hint of the mountain smell that often flows with it. The Poudre starts up near the continental divide at thirteen-thousand feet of elevation in Rocky Mountain National Park, and when the wind's just right, you can smell the ponderosa pine, and even the high-elevation lodgepole pine, all the way down the canyon and here in Fort Collins. The closer my face gets to the water, the more I can smell it, and the better I feel.

A few moments later, when I suggest that it's time to leave, Julia asks me this, "Dad, can we go over to McMurray Pond?" She's referring to a five-acre pond about a hundred yards upstream. We often go there with the canoe and paddle around, or we swim or watch wildlife. Once, a year ago, we watched a mother and kitten beaver swim circles in the pond as we paddled nearby.

I think for a second about all the other things I ought to be doing. And then I answer, "Sure we can, Julia."

She asks, "Can we walk all the way in the river?"

I pause, and then shoot back, "You bet."

And then we walk upstream, against the current, and I see her lean forward, into it.

"Lean," I think to myself. "Move those legs. That's the way to get where you want. That's the only way change ever happens."

# Haiku
Tim Vaughan

*Tim Vaughan has traveled the West as a geologist and now resides in Fort Collins, near the Cache la Poudre River. Haiku, which Tim offers below and has written for years, consists of seventeen syllables organized into three lines of five, seven, and five syllables. In the tradition of this Japanese form, Tim presents a vivid emotion or image of nature which urges the reader toward reflection and insight.*

**January on the Poudre**
two feet balancing
on water worn cobblestones
my face turns sunward

**August**
this still eve I sense
the Poudre's suffering and
I read her poetry

**Dippers in October**
bob and weave dancers
shoot the rapid, eddy out
god's entertainment

**Hayden Looks Toward the Poudre**
his eyes turn eastward
where smaller ridges die out
like waves on the sea

**Brinks Place**
a crouched girl searches
for the Cache de la Poudre
in her memory

**May**
fox eyes follow them
across murky backwaters
ducklings trailing mom

# Heart of the River
## Paul Miller

*Paul Miller is a writer and editor in Fort Collins whose creative non-fiction has appeared in national and local publications and several literary anthologies. Here, he gives us a story of a troubled family—good friends of his—whose son's problems reflect the turmoil Paul has experienced at times in his own life. Paul hopes the river will offer the boy the same healing that it offered him.*

Nate, the thirteen-year-old son of my great, good friend, is knee-deep in the Cache la Poudre River, trying to skip stones across the grain of the swift current. His thin arms and legs are pale in the glare of the hot afternoon, in the quick breath of wind, in the deep voice of the water. Nate's busy at work, setting loose stones in a row on the dry crease of a half-submerged boulder, carefully choosing the next rock, the one that just may skip forever. His best effort, though, barely produces two skips before the rock vanishes. He tries another, and another. The river seems hungry for more, chasing down the stones and pulling them under. The water is as energized as this boy, this skinny kid who's visiting from a Great Lakes city, who's never seen the mountains where this cold water is born.

Nate ranges upriver and down a few dozen yards, wild hair pushed under a baseball hat, fashionable sunglasses hiding his eyes. The bottom few inches of his baggy shorts are wet, but he doesn't care. Watching him from the shade of sturdy ponderosas, his parents flanking me, I can't help thinking how innocent he looks, all loose limbs and energy. Nate grins at some private joke, a small wind brushes the willows on the bank, and I think about the damage this young teenager has caused in the life of his family.

Nate's father, Bill, my friend of many decades, has become more and more subdued, sometimes morose, over the past few years. Not long ago, he told me a story about how a man he knew confronted him in the neighborhood. Bill was walking down the sidewalk. The neighbor drove up slowly in his car. He leaned out the window and yelled at Bill about some abomination Nate committed, some crime against another kid that Bill couldn't remember ten minutes later, he'd heard it so often before from other people. "So here's this guy, all red in the face, yelling and threatening me and Nate and the whole family," Bill said. "He kept at it for quite a while, but I didn't hear much of anything he was saying after the first few words."

Nobody is cavalier about Nate's problems, not his mother, not Bill. Bill tells another story that infuriates him, about how he had to almost bribe the school to let his son go on an out-of-state field trip for a weekend. "For two days after the buses leave, I don't hear anything. No phone call, no frantic message from a chaperone. We're hoping for the best. Maybe this time, things will be okay. Then it's the end of the field trip, the bus rolls up in the parking lot, and there's Nate, sitting all by himself in the front seat near the driver. Something happened, and I heard about that, too."

Nate likes to torment other kids until they lash out at him, then he hits back. Or he just skips the first step and hits kids. Nobody's really sure why. Nate won't say anything—the worse trouble he's in, the less he says. Over the years, he's been to doctors, counselors, church school, therapists, a school for special-needs children. He's so smart it's scary, more than willing to learn math or how to cane a chair or run a sewing machine, as long as an adult whom he happens to like shows him how. Some adults, he can handle. For a little while. Bill's admitted to me that he almost hurt his son once, seriously hurt him. His eyes welled up remembering, and he fell silent for a long time.

————

Boats full of paddlers in blue helmets and cheap yellow parkas come down the Poudre. The guides at the back of the boats yell instructions to the crews, and in haphazard unison the crews paddle, sending the rafts into a froth of clashing oars, a line of rubber bumper cars rocking down the river. I wonder if Nate would like to try a short raft trip. I've rafted this river a dozen times or more—for years, I've lived a mere twenty minutes from this spot—and the cold water alone tends to re-arrange your scruples, makes you remember how sweet life is. Maybe he'd love it and become a tanned, sinewy river guide and spend his life rigging rafts, floating indolently down water so remote that eagles get lost, drinking bouquets of river scenery, sleeping on narrow sand beaches or rimrock, wearing the same shorts and T-shirt until the cloth gives up.

I can only hope that's what will suit his temperament, to range out like some feral but benign backcountry madman, an outdoor genius who comes into town only long enough to pick up some yeast and mo-lasses. It could be the urban living that makes him crazy, makes him lash out with his fists, enraged about all the annoying crap he is required to perform like a trained animal. That much I can understand. I live and work in urban environments, and I've been tempted to hit people, too. Maybe I'm piling my own dreams and delusions onto Nate, seeing him permanently escape into some made-up, backcountry nirvana of blue sky and wild berries, like I wish I had done when I was a teenager. I don't even have kids of my own to pour my dreams into, like some rare metal into a mold.

Bill may well be unloading his own escapist dreams onto Nate, too. I know that's one thing eating at Bill, this overloaded urban nausea we live in. For decades, Bill's tried finding other work so he can get away from the tire industry, a career he started not long after high school. He's conjured up one scheme after another, from selling recumbent bi-cycles out of his house to starting a landscaping company, but nothing has ever worked out.

On another river three years ago, Bill was an altogether different human being. Four short days on the Colorado River, through Cataract Canyon, and we all managed to forget what day of the week it was. No watches, no cellphones, no bugs, no rain, no shoes. Millions of stars kept us company, and wide beaches, and baking sandstone, and the silt-laden river murmuring day and night, the sweetest sound on the planet. Bill ran rapids like a pro, hiked to Anasazi ruins in sandals, lifted va-porous toasts to bats working the endless evening sky, ate hearty meals, slept like a dead man. He cuts an imposing figure, over six feet tall, bald head, dark eyes that bore into you, and when he's in the depths of conversation, you want to hear what he has to say next. He makes you say more intelligent things just so you can hold his interest.

He couldn't stop talking about it, our brief trip down the Colorado, couldn't stop thinking about it when he got back home to his messy stifling home in the Midwest, to a job that wasn't getting any better, a son who kept getting worse. He wanted more, dreaming out loud about spending fourteen days rafting through the Grand Canyon, a week and a half on the Yampa, twenty years anywhere. For four days, he'd lived with the Colorado River, with the laughter and bullshit of a bunch of sun-baked people, and saw maybe for the first time what this planet had to offer, the grit of the landscape, the priceless paintings of desert varnish, the roiling water that washes your soul clean every time a wave comes up and smacks you in the face.

———

Back on the Poudre, on this hot July day, I peel off everything but my shorts and submerge myself in a small eddy swirling snowmelt around like a blender. Shocking, electrifying, like having your skin taken off and replaced with a tighter, cleaner shell. Bill indulges up to his waist but declines the full baptismal service. He watches Nate, close enough to hear a young girl admire his son's sandals. Nate doesn't care much about girls, but that soon will change, I think. For now, he'd rather skip stones. I consider joining him. I'm still a stone skipper and tree climber, even at my age, more than 50 years and counting.

What's going to happen to this kid? But then, why am I still asking the question? When I was in my early teens, my parents probably were close to giving up on me, as devoted as I was to making their lives miserable. My mother wept, more than once, trying to get me to do something as simple as talk to her. My father, who believed in sound beatings, probably was tempted to keep on hitting me until nothing was left. It's easy for me, for Bill, for teachers and neighbors, to see Nate as somehow permanently broken, but I remember how long it took me to straighten out, an embarrassing amount of time. I never got into the habit of hitting people, but I still wasn't pleasant to be around until I moved away and started ranging out where nobody—and nothing—was willing to put up with some gloomy twerp. Even then, it took a couple of tries.

The first time, I was in my early twenties, living in my boyhood home in the thick air of north-central Ohio, sick of the grind of industrial work, choking on the claustrophobia of living with a family who seemed satisfied with nothing ever changing. After a few months of thinking about it, I spent a summer afternoon packing the trunk of a VW bug with everything I owned, drove down the street lined with people I'd grown up with, and headed west across the baking breadbasket of the country, fueled by notions of vagabond glory I'd read about in John Steinbeck and the Beat writers.

I rolled right into the spine of the Rockies, lay flat on my back for days watching thunderheads boiling miles into the sky. I stood with toes dangling over the edge of a cliff at Bryce Canyon, where hoodoo spires stood like sentinels in the dry wind. I touched the base of granite monoliths in Yosemite, wandered around the edges of Los Angeles, slept outside the entrance gate of the Petrified Forest in Arizona until park rangers discovered me in the morning and dressed me down for breaking the rules, but who allowed me to tour the park anyway. I picked up a crazy but well-meaning man from France who was thumbing by the side of the road, and drove with him all the way to New Orleans, where we spent two days with a crazy and annoying woman who, bless her, knew some herbal remedies to help me get rid of a bad rash of poison ivy I'd caught in California. The herbs helped, but not as much as soaking in the salt water of the Gulf of Mexico near Pensacola, Florida.

After months on the road, I made my way home, thinking that, as sated and road-weary as I was, I'd be able to live with my family in peace, smoking my pipe and telling tales of the wandering life like some new-age Kerouac.

I smoked my pipe, certainly, filling it more with weed than tobacco, but the stories I told turned hackneyed to my ears even as I was telling them. Something still wasn't right, some deep dissatisfaction I couldn't escape, some kink in my soul that kept me wary of the people I met and the strange, wondrous landscape, so vast and tumbling and careless that I felt crushed under the weight of it all.

So I went back to my job at the sheet-metal plant, not having learned enough to stay away from it, and spent years drowning in toxins, brooding about how unfair it all was, just trying to live like a human being but getting kicked around like a dog. Such self-indulgence went on and on until I grew sick of it, sick of the continuous-loop tape running in my head that blamed everyone else for misery of my own devising.

There was no defining moment, no revelation that came dancing out of the clouds that finally stopped the tape. Maybe it was just growing older, or some rogue gene from a great uncle kicking in, or the thought of facing another sultry summer in Ohio, but I felt the need again for movement, for ranging out into new places on my own and worrying about nothing more than how to feed myself, to walk down some strange street and know that nobody would have any idea who I was.

I cooked up another scheme, and this one worked. In the late 1970s, I loaded everything I owned onto a passenger train, moved wholesale to Colorado, and managed to invent myself all over again. Very nearly—internal baggage is hard to get rid of, and I towed enough dis-ease along to make me wobble at times—but the small town where I moved, tucked up hard against the central Rockies, showed me what stuffing I was made of. At first I ranged around on an old bicycle, then worked enough odd jobs to buy a ten-year-old car. I started driving into the heart of the mountains, daring them to teach me a lesson.

And, fortune of all good fortune, I've been learning ever since.

———

I stand in the Cache la Poudre River up to my thighs, glistening drops falling off my arms. The river instantly sweeps clean its surface where the drops fall. Ponderosa and willow crowd down to the edge, and the hillside is covered with larkspur, chokecherry, mountain mahogany, rock clematis, wild rose, three-leaf sumac. From my stance, with the current tugging, teasing, compelling me to slide in, to let go, to ricochet downstream, I can see upriver where the Poudre disappears around a corner, one of dozens, hundreds of mysteries that never will be solved. What does this cold, tumbling river look like fifty feet upstream? Two hundred yards? Six miles? What animal bones lie in secret grottos, what rotted planks from old water courses feed the vegetation in some nameless canyon?

I know what the Poudre looks like and how it tastes at one of its sources, high in Rocky Mountain National Park. Every time I think about seeing it for the first time many long years ago, I'm right back there again, hiking northeast through Flint Pass, just short of where the South Fork of the Poudre is born. It's 1982, and I'm on well-used paths made by elk and deer, the only trails that go through the pass. Dense, low-growing thickets of willow scrape my legs as I add my footprints to the hoof marks, some deep enough to carry small reservoirs of muddy, scat-laced water. I have only one more night left in a wandering four-day backcountry tour, and I'm headed toward a site I'm not sure about.

I've only seen this area before on a topographic map, but now, with the landscape alive all around me, I'm already vowing to return. Up ahead, Flint Pass flattens out to become a wind funnel, smack between the huge flank of Rowe Mountain on the right and a much smaller pile of rock on the left. At the pass, I stand for a long time looking down at a broad, open valley, some 11,400 feet in elevation, as thunderheads build and the wind picks up, dampening my legs and arms with a sheen of atomized rain. I still have to descend and hike across the valley, then find somewhere to pitch a tent, maybe at timberline near where the South Fork becomes big enough to name. I start heading down, but then a motion catches my eye, and I stop and stand still until a white-tailed ptarmigan emerges like a magic act out of the surrounding terrain, plumage so closely matching the lichen-encrusted rocks that I'm afraid to move for fear of stepping on another bird I can't see.

We regard each other. The plump grouse's head twitches slightly, and I shift my weight from one foot to the other. I'd like to stand here for hours, sharing silent stories with the bird, but thunder rolls behind me from lightning I can't see, and I have to move on before the weather worsens. I don't have the same ability to shed rain as the ptarmigan, but then, I don't have the same responsibilities as the bird, as I discover. I move slowly around her, then abruptly stop again. Not two feet away are her chicks, tiny balls of feathers with dark eyes. They're so close together that I can't tell how many there are, but I don't stay to find out.

It's tough enough to be a newborn up here in the krummholz without some big smelly monster stomping around, so I back off, reversing my steps until I'm a few dozen yards away. I give the birds wide latitude, and continue down into the valley.

A few hours later, I settle into a site in some wind-driven trees, within earshot of the South Fork, a small but forceful stream, a water-bearing gravity machine falling away into dense wood and brush and steep canyons. That night, a tremendous thunderstorm passes right overhead, thunder shaking the ground while I lie in my tent, clinging to mortality, bolts of lightning striking so close I'm deafened from the concussion. Rain pummels the ground and smacks the tent until I swear I've come unmoored and am drifting down the valley toward the river, to join the rushing waters, another piece of flotsam to catch and break loose and catch again. After twenty minutes—or several days, I can't be sure—the storm moves off, and I check to make sure my ears aren't bleeding and nothing is burned. I wonder how the ptarmigan family is doing, and fight the urge to range out in the darkness to find out, to see if I can even come close to locating the nest again. I fall asleep instead, trusting the birds to know what to do.

The morning comes dense with fog. I pack up my sodden gear and head up a steep slope to Mummy Pass Trail, exhilarated by my own movement, by deep draughts of thin air, by the fog wrapped around me like a gauze curtain. Although I can't see more than a few dozen yards, I can hear the river to my right, the tumbling water gathering more volume as it drops, born in this high place of cold trickles and long winters and spare, sturdy life. Nothing else matters but that sweet sound.

The heart of the river carries me all the way home.

————

Nate's in the backseat of the car, a baking oven on four wheels. We're still damp from the river, which helps ease the suffocating heat. Bill's beside me, brooding, running his hands over his face as if trying to wash away some torment. Does he regret that he never joined Nate skipping stones in the Poudre? I should ask Bill what's bugging him, if there's some other worry bigger than his son, but the opportunity never presents itself. I've listened to him for years, and I know he'll figure it out somehow. If he doesn't, maybe another river will do the trick. There must be another river, always.

I start the car, drive down the canyon. Nate is pattering in the back, full of silly noise. All the rest of us are silent, as if we're holding our breaths, waiting for Nate to recover from a deep fever. I'm afraid his nameless rage will continue for too many years, until he sees something much bigger than himself, something that shakes him to the core.

I look at him in the rearview mirror, his blond hair a messy bird's nest, and I'm seized with the impulse to turn around and drop him off at the river's edge, as far up the canyon as I can. I'll give him a knife, a small raft, and a bandana for his particulars, and tell him to take his time coming back, maybe a few months, long enough to inhale the fear of a thunderstorm or the first flight of a bird winging into the wind over some wide lost alpine meadow.

I'll watch until this skinny kid sets off downstream and disappears, the river reaching up and pulling him home, blessing all the years he has yet to live.

# Memoir
Evan Oakley

*Evan Oakley teaches at Aims Community College in Greeley,
Colorado. His poetry has appeared in many publications, including*
North American Review *and other anthologies. For many years, he
codirected Loveland, Colorado's annual "Poets in the Park" festival,
which featured many nationally famous poets. In his poem below,
Evan reflects on his hearing disability and how the Poudre has spoken
to him in a different sensory form.*

Deaf One, you went alone to the parties,
beside the Poudre, beside trashfires,
where the chrome of motorcycles
babbled orange in darkness.
The river stones were like you,

unhearing. A girl's dog lapped
wine from a hubcap, and she
laughed, holding him. The radios
of parked cars delivered lyrics
into the naked trees & all they had

you asked for. Mishawaka twinkled
in party-light hues while you sprawled
on carhoods, feeling in your sternum
the bass, pretending to yourself it was
the experience of music.

Came the midnight when laughter
fell on things, and the things vanished.
Bottles winked into water. A shotgun
snapped candy-colored shells
into the bore, and opened

on the river's face with a flame.
Others seemed to be smiling,
and you mouthed what you saw
on their faces, throwing your hair
until the blood pounded like sound.

# Godzilla at the River
## Laura Pritchett

*Laura Pritchett grew up along the banks of the Cache la Poudre on a small ranch and now lives a few miles up-river. She is the author of a novel,* Sky Bridge, *and a collection of short stories,* Hell's Bottom, Colorado, *and her work has appeared in numerous places, including* The Sun, Orion, High Country News, *and* 5280. *Her work often focuses on land-use issues and ranchland preservation in the West. "Godzilla at the River" recounts her most difficult battle to date, that with an unexpected monster, on the banks of the Cache.*

> *Our bodies are molded rivers.*
> —Novalis

The Cache la Poudre River attracts ceremony. No surprise here—all rivers do. But the Cache is my river, and when I meander along its banks these days, I never fail to stumble into evidence of art and ritual, of solemn and playful rites.

On one sandy beach, I frequently find this: Yellow cornmeal sprinkled in a circle with deep-red rose petals scattered on the inside. Footprints all around—someone has been dancing! I imagine that she comes here in the very early morning to beckon in the day.

In another place, I've discovered piles of large, stacked river rocks. Perhaps thirty vertical columns of stone—orbs piled one atop the other, in descending size as they rise, like stalagmites grown from the earth. They are balanced so carefully, so high: This has been a labor- and time-intensive project, and I wonder what soul has been out here, what drives him to create these wonders.

I have seen dozens of stone designs in the sand: circles, swoops, rocks of the same color lined up, circled round. Sometimes these rock designs are made on the beach, some in the river itself. Black rocks forming a fish-design, for instance, barely discernable beneath the water.

In a hidden-away spot near my home, where the river runs next to a cliff, someone has made a miniature village in a small cave. Clay people, buildings, fences, animals. I cross the river and check on this village from time to time, see it get a little more weathered, the animals and people toppled over.

I've seen sand angels like snow angels, sand castles, sand ditches, stick shelters, stone paths across the river, words written in sand.

I like to think of all these things as evidence of some sort of ceremony. They are created not for the river, but for the people, who, perhaps, want to play, to pray, or to heal.

———

It started simply enough. An ache in my arm turned electric—currents that zinged back and forth, sometimes with a force that was just annoying and sometimes with enough energy to make me dizzy. The doctor put my hand in a splint, sent me to physical therapy. "Myofacial pain, median nerve neuropathy" was the first diagnosis.

This was in March, right between winter and spring, and both my body and the seasons shifted. I took a lot of Tylenol, started reading up on stretching, posture, ergonomics. My kids—Jake, age five, and Ellie, age three—began doing more things for themselves. I quit writing. I used my left hand whenever possible. I took walks along the river, bundled up against the still-cold air, my feet wet with snow. I had a large reservoir of patience and strength, from easy and pleasant times previous, so I wasn't worried or beleaguered. I simply waited for healing.

———

Most of my life has been spent along the banks of the Cache la Poudre. I grew up on a ranch that borders the river, playing with my brothers, sitting alone, chasing cows, riding horses, fishing. I've found some of the river's most beautiful rocks, caught trout from its banks, inner-tubed down its rapids, rafted other parts. I've hiked its banks, gone to its reservoirs, walked across it to school, kissed boyfriends on its beaches, gotten drunk on its shores, smashed its winter ice with my feet, thrown a thousand rocks into its waters. The Cache is as much a part of my internal landscape as are the other essentials of my life: family, books, nature, loves.

As an adult, I've settled down a half-mile upstream. I go to this river constantly: to play, to sit, to walk. I've made life-decisions on its banks, thought up short stories and worked out plots for novels, played with my kids, stared at the sky. It's often where I go when I need to find the core of myself, or when I need help.

———

The pain started to arc up in my body with ferocious energy. It came quickly and with gasp-producing force. Pinched nerve, I thought, and called a neck specialist. Two MRIs showed nothing much—some stenosis, a narrowing of the spinal column, and some mild scoliosis. An EMG—a test where electricity is shot up the nerves of the arm to check for damage—didn't show much either.

I quit typing completely, started reading books with promising titles like *Pain Free* and *Life Without Pain*. I snorted in delight at the new geeky stretches I was doing: strange contortions with my nose against a wall, toes pointed together, arms stretched above. I started learning things about the neuromuscular system, different kinds of therapies, specialists, medications. New words entered my vocabulary: Thoracic Outlet Syndrome, ulnar entrapment, carpal tunnel.

My arm felt as if I'd grabbed an electrical fence and couldn't let go. I tried to be in a good mood about it, but in truth, I would have chopped off my arm if that would've solved the problem. I was often close to passing out. The orthopedic doc put a cast on it. I took pain meds and waited.

I stayed flat on my back and played with my daughter. I told my son stories about sword-fights instead of actually engaging in one. The house started to fall apart. Meetings and appointments were canceled and e-mails sent warning of work delays. I told my publicist I couldn't travel to promote my new novel.

No worries, I told myself. Small glitch, part of life, no use complaining, nothing compared to what other people sometimes suffer through. This is nothing.

———

*Ceremony* is thought to be derived from a Sanskrit word, *karma*, which implies that acts and behaviors should be well thought out because of their inevitable consequences in the future. For centuries, water has been an essential part of ceremony. There is something about water that makes us consider our lives and actions—probably because we are so fundamentally dependent on it—and I would guess that we build ceremonies around this substance more than any other.

Until the Middle Ages, people regarded rivers, lakes, and oceans as being alive and possessing spirits. The Celts carried over these notions into Christianity, holding that all nature, especially water, was penetrated by the spirit of God. Hindus trek to the Indus River, Judeo-Christians dunk their own under, and Amazonian shamanic healers practice their arts at their own rivers. In Navajo healing ceremonies, a sand painting is done at a river, which is to be destroyed before dawn. Here in my hometown, there's a newspaper article this week—a professor memorializes a dead student by building a stone arrangement under the waters of the Cache. All over the world, we go to rivers to pray, to heal.

I am not a churchgoer anymore, but I would call the river, and the mountains around it, my holy place. I *do* believe in the importance of ritual and ceremony. I believe that they can convey knowledge that words cannot; they conjure emotions that otherwise are buried. It was during this time, during this pain, that I started thinking about my own ceremonies, and my need to heal next to this river.

———

Pain has a life of its own, and my pain began a new life course. It began to radiate in strange ways, in rivulets down both arms, leaving numb or tingly sensations behind it. I couldn't straighten my fingers, and when

I did, my whole hand shook. My hand was cold, then tingly hot. Weeks went on, different drugs, different attempts to figure out the cause.

The pain kept me awake, and I was exhausted. I couldn't remember things, plan things, do things. I couldn't form sentences without faltering. I kept my mouth closed, so that people wouldn't know.

There's something else about pain, too: When it can't be released, when it doesn't let up, it starts to make you crazy. I would bury my head into a pillow and scream, then stand and bonk my head into a wall. I shook and panted and paced. My brain spun itself into confused realms, and my thoughts did not come, and when they did, they seemed too dark, too nonsensical, too evil to be mine.

The bills piled up. The medical folder, once so thin, was now packed full. My husband was harried—trying to do his work and mine. My daughter had dreams that bugs were eating her back and arm, and my son asked if I'd ever, ever be able to play again. I started to sink into silence.

Then something new: I started feeling like my nervous system had been poisoned—I felt adrenaline rushes constantly—as if I were caught in a raging river, in danger of being pounded by rocks and the force of the water itself. My heart raced, my skin poured out sweat. I wanted to fight something, but there was nothing to fight. I wanted to flee, but there was nowhere to go. My thoughts were too fast, confused.

Maybe I was going crazy, or dying, or both. My mind used to be my best friend—it occupied me, consoled me, conducted endless threads of thought on philosophy and human behavior, and I was endlessly entertained with its stories. Now my mind was slow and stupid, and I began to hate it. I hated my body, too, and I lost so much weight that the scale read what it did way back in high school.

Only later did I learn that the physical symptoms were plain old anxiety—a nervous system in a crazed state. At the time, I thought I literally had been poisoned by some toxin, drug, chemical. Indeed, my body had—by its own overproduction of cortisone and adrenaline, the hormones of stress.

I went to the river, sat on its beaches, and talked myself out of the deepening gloom. I tried to breathe in additional resistance and patience, I tried not to get scared. I tried to see my body like a river. My body was a river that had all sorts of things flowing through it, things that flow and do not stagnate, and in their flowing, they are released, and therefore, the hurt would someday be gone. But I also knew I was starting to sink.

––––––––

The town I grew up in, and now reside near, is named LaPorte. *La porte* is French for "the door" or "behold the gate"—a gift from the first French trappers, who prized this valley since it rested near an entryway into the Rocky Mountains. It's this river that did it, that carved a door through blue peaks—perhaps it's hard for us to think now of how important, and difficult, finding a pathway up into the mountains could be.

They named this river that gives us a door to the mountains the *Cache la Poudre*. Cache of powder. In one story, a caravan of trappers and travelers were attacked by Indians. In another, the travelers simply needed to lighten the load. In either case, legend has it, they buried their extra guns and gunpowder somewhere around here. *Cache la poudre*.

In the 1860s, LaPorte had four saloons, a brewery, a butcher shop, a shoe shop, two blacksmith shops, a store, and a hotel. The town housed trappers, traders, Indians, the military, the Overland Trail Stage Station, the County Courthouse; LaPorte was the biggest settlement north of Denver. It was an important place to stop on the journey along the Overland Trail.

All because of this river.

I have looked for the cache my whole life, but the river offered other treasures instead: old nails, blue bottles, foundations of old stone houses, a cable that was used for the ferry crossing. I found all sorts of things, but mainly I found a place on earth I could go to and feel alone but not lonely, where I could be curious, thoughtful, quiet, happy.

––––––––

Suddenly I realized that doctors and friends were suggesting things that were not *structural* in nature, not orthopedic—they were suggesting diseases. New words came up: fibromyalgia, West Nile virus, lupus, rheumatoid arthritis, peripheral neuropathy, Reflex Empathetic Dystrophy, MS. My sister sent me an article about a woman who had Lyme disease but got diagnosed with MS, and had the Lyme part of the problem undiagnosed for years. Her symptoms sounded exactly like mine—arm pain, neuropathic pain, strange numbness. Another friend told an opposite story: A woman was told she likely had MS, but it turned out to be a miniscule disc fragment that had been knocking against a nerve in her spine. I also heard many stories of people with similar nerve pain that was *never* explained by neurologists. I realized that the body is still quite a mystery, and the nervous system perhaps the biggest mystery of all.

I wanted to arch away from my own physical self. This body I've loved, been comfortable with, befriended. I understood, for the first time, the misery of being stuck in the confines of a body. I realized what people mean when they say that the body is no place to live.

––––––––

Human beings are made up mostly of water, in roughly the same percentage as water is to the surface of the earth. Our tissues, hearts, sweat, tears, membranes are formed mainly of oxygen (61%) and hydrogen (10%), fused together in the unique molecular combination known as water. Our brains are three-quarters water—hardly anything else—and yet within this organ is the ability to try to comprehend itself. This watery mass is the origin of joy, and the origin of pain.

Of all the water that exists on Earth—326,000,000 cubic miles—less than 3 percent is fresh, and most of it is locked in icecaps and glaciers. The Cache la Poudre is a vessel that carries a tiny amount of fresh water, and my body is a vessel that carries a smaller part of this river's waters. But how big we can seem, from this small perspective.

There is great power in rivers—the way they take hold in the mind. Can anyone stare into a river and not get mesmerized? Water is a magnet for the imagination, it allows the brain to ponder, to seek. It is familiar, because it is sacred to our life, and because it is us.

I dipped my toes into the freezing snow-melt and stared, and was mesmerized by the condition of my life and body. I scraped at the sand with my fingernails, digging into the earth as far as I could before my fingers felt raw, begging the water of my body to flow more calmly.

———

I've always wanted to see what my brain looks like.

When the electricity started zinging down my spine, I went in for my fourth MRI, this one of the brain. It's true I was a little excited—perhaps because I believe my brain *is* me. There resides the essence, thoughts, emotions, loves, fears, memories, and dreams of Laura.

And there it was: curves of brain material, strange loops, very much like the photos of other brains, but as I studied it, I came to believe it was unique in its own folds. Yet the report, thankfully, read, "This brain is unremarkable." Which is exactly what I wanted to hear—that I was only and wonderfully unremarkable.

The pain and anxiety persisted. The acupuncturist stabbed in needles. The chiropractor cracked my neck. The kinesiologist said I had sensitivity to wheat germ. The neuromuscular-reeducation-massage specialist talked to me about breathing, posture, and eating avocados. The biofeedback machine told me that my adrenal glands and digestive system were out of whack, and I got talked into buying evening primrose oil and deep ocean whitefish tablets. The family doctor told me to take Cymbalta to cut down on neuropathic pain, which made my body agitated. The massage therapist worked away, releasing muscles in my neck. The physical therapist pulled down on my first rib and pulled sideways on my vertebrae, trying to realign my spine. The neurologist, the second neurologist, the arm specialist, and the neck specialist told me that they didn't know and that they were sorry. The visceral manipulation person "released my kidneys," moving them from my pelvis to where they're supposed to be, under the rib cage. The therapist told me to push on a rubber ball to get rid of my negative emotions. Another psychologist started teaching me about cognitive behavioral strategies and coping with difficult times.

I was confronting my body in new ways, with lightning speed, as fast as the currents running down my neck and arm. I felt like I was trying so hard—what else, in the end, could I do?

My parents re-entered my life—as caretakers, once again. They brought me roses and drove me to doctor appointments, watched my kids, and when they got frustrated, told me to Buck Up. My mom did research on the Internet, my dad told me to have a glass of milk each night. My brothers patted me on the back, instead of punching me in the arm as usual, and tilted their heads in concerned ways. Friends brought over food. Strangers told me they were praying for me. Other friends gave advice on good neurologists and pain medications—friends with worse problems than mine, who unfortunately knew the ins-and-outs of the local medical system because of necessity—and I felt ridiculous for bothering them, and felt increased sorrow at their pain.

Each offering brought a tide of new tears. Perhaps because I was so grateful, perhaps because I was so fragile, perhaps because their kindnesses made me feel so raw, so needy, so helpless.

I started to seriously consider the unthinkable: How would my husband manage with the kids by himself? How would my kids fare without a mother? If faced with death, was I ready to go? What loose ends did I need to take care of? And if … if this pain persisted like this, was I willing to take my own life? And if so, where, and how, and when?

The rational part of my brain knew I wasn't going to die of a painful arm and back, or even of the panic attacks that felt so much like my body was falling apart. But the pain itself was taking away reason. It was just this: I knew I didn't want my life to go on in this way. I wasn't strong enough, could not endure it forever, or perhaps even very long.

I stared into the river, which was at its highest now, full with snowmelt and tumbling down with its greatest force, and I realized how desperate I was.

———

Once, when I was a girl, perhaps nine or so, I was walking across the spillway on my parents' ranch. The spillway is a large cement structure—a small dam—that crosses the river and diverts some of the flow to ditches. I had been playing out there for an hour or more, probably stabbing the silky moss that grows on the cement. Or watching fish. Or searching for gold.

I didn't notice that the river had risen—it often would, as the water got released from the reservoir above. As I started to walk back to shore, I realized that the water had risen to my mid-calf, and it was fast. Fast enough that I had to place each step carefully before I shifted my weight, or the force of the water would have washed me down the spillway.

I cried because I was scared. Because I was caught in water that was rising and because it was dangerous. I was young enough and naïve enough that I had not yet realized the power of water, how it could turn from a friend to foe. I knew that if it knocked me off balance and I tumbled down the cement curve, I would be hurt badly. I placed each step carefully, with great attention, and with great fear. It took such a long time to get across the spillway, only thirty feet or so, that my legs were exhausted from the effort when I finally scrambled up the opposite bank.

I didn't go back out on the spillway for a long time. The body remembers fear.

———

"Pretend your anxiety is a monster, perhaps Godzilla," advised one book. "Yell at it. Tell it to go away, that it doesn't have control over your life."

So in the mornings, when I woke to a racing heart, sweat drenching my body, tingling arms and legs, lungs that weren't getting enough oxygen, I yelled at Godzilla. I walked to the river and yelled. Cortisone, the chemical of stress, is at its peak in the morning, and I came to understand that if I walked it off in the morning, cried it out of my body, I could be mainly rid of it for the day. I walked and walked, for miles.

I went to the river at my parents' ranch, stood by the spillway, hidden by water noise and trees, and yelled.

I went to Watson Lake, sat on the beach, stared at the river.

I went up the canyon, to my two favorite secret spots, rested my cheek on the beach and stared at the sand granules in front of my eyes.

I saw the "June Rise," as people call it—when the river rises from all the snowmelt and suddenly becomes a wild, alive thing again. This year, there was more water than I had seen for years, and this year, I paid attention as never before. I noticed the pasque flowers, always the first out, with more appreciation. I watched the new growth of spring first emerge from soil, then spread and grow and increase until the world again began to look green. Flowers unfolded, pinecones dropped and new ones formed, birds returned.

It was during these trips that I saw other bits of evidence of other people's gestures and ceremonies. Healing or spiritual or prayerful—I don't know. Piles of rocks. Circles of corn powder. Designs of rock very much like my own. I also found beer bottles, cigarette butts, drug paraphernalia. I think those were all evidence of an attempt at healing, too.

————

The pain slowly started to subside. I don't know which of the therapies was helping, or if it was just time, or a combination of them all. Soon I could move around pretty well. My neck muscles loosened. With the shrinking pain, and the decrease in medication, the anxiety started to lessen. There was still pain, but not the excruciating sort, and thus I could think, and find reason.

I called my publicist and restarted part of the book tour I had canceled. I watched funny movies. I started to meditate. I practiced yoga and tai chi. I played a lot with my kids. Cleaned the house. Caught up on e-mails. Cooked a meal or two. Spring turned to summer and slowly, slowly, pain eroded and my spirits and energy rose.

These days, the pain is not so bad, and mostly I just feel raw. A little too sensitive to the hurt of the world, like I still need to close up and mend. I wake up each morning with a fear that the hurt is going to descend again; and any time I do feel the pain increase, panic sets in. I find myself thinking melodramatic thoughts: *If I can just make it till the kids are at least seven. … Good, at least one more good day with the kids, one more meal served, one more load of laundry done. … Please let this beautiful moment in the pine trees not be the last.*

The physical therapist is able to gently pull and crack and crunch my bones apart, sideways, and together. He has come to know the curves of my spine, and his hands can feel out the nerve bundles connected to them. When I leave his office, I swing my neck around gently, delighted by the range of motion, and then I smile. I'm so grateful to be me again, molded water, bound by skin, the inside mostly healed.

————

Water has a skin of its own. We see insects race across it; we break it when we place a finger into its surface. If we concentrate, we can almost feel it.

Where air meets water—this is the skin of water. It is only one molecule thick, and is formed by a special arrangement of molecules that switch back and forth to form this layer. Unlike any other substance, the skin is made from the same elements as that which it encloses. It is only that the water molecules are more attracted to each other than they are to the air, so the molecules underneath the surface pull more strongly, heaving some molecules in, pushing others out. This minuscule layer has a tensile strength that is equal to that of steel.

I went to the river yesterday to feel the skin of the Cache. I piled up white rocks—a ceremony that means nothing to anyone except me. My finger wrote "thank you" in the sand, and I said "thank you" out loud. Perhaps because the river's going to keep going, because it's more constant and sure than I am, because it has a force and a strength that will outlast mine, and because its body offered mine what it could.

# The Soul Is a River,
# The River Has a Soul
## Clarissa Pinkola Estés

*Clarissa Pinkola Estés drove the Pan American Highway from Denver to South America in the 1960s, meeting thieves,* borrachos, *bureaucracies, and seeing the effect of two horrific guerrilla wars—and thereby fulfilled her childhood quest to stand at the headwaters of the Amazon. Estés grew up near the bend of the St. Joseph River, a broad tributary of the Mississippi. When she migrated to the Sangre de Cristos and thence to the Rockies, she walked miles of canyons and rivers, including the Cache la Poudre. In one of her books, she writes, "What constitutes integrity of love for land, water, sky and the soul in all things? I think integral love means to develop 'el ojo tonal,' a kind of 'long eye,' which, in part, means to devote oneself to envisioning what our great-grandchildren will see, hear, and know of the soul if we act now, or what our great-grandchildren will see, hear, and know of the soul if we do not act now. ... There is a duty that arises from the far-seeing soul ... to allow and protect in all things within our reach, the kind of wild beauty that is friendly, but never tame."*

I
*El rio abajo el rio,*
there is a River beneath the river,
one that can never be destroyed....

From 'the river beneath the river,'
I learnt to leap and keep going,
to catch the verve of shout places,
and if escape be needed,
to make myself fine as mist.
I learnt from rivers, that going to the edges
will lead to Plato's cave,

that slots filled with debris often hold
the oldest grandfather trout,
and that the middle of the river
like the middle of so much in life,
is often not the deepest.

From dams, after an hour's pacing
atop those concrete shoulders,
there I learnt staidness and sameness,
and that seamless look that never changes
and holds the heart far back.

If it's passion and vision,
invention and inoculation
I've needed,
I go to the rivers.

And for the ways of metal and mechanics
I remember the dams.

II
As a child, I was taken to Hoover dam,
one of the wonders of the world, they said,
and in a way it was, a testament to the workers
who risked their lives to build a concrete moat
complete with castlettes
to hold back the Mother water,
and all the life she once nourished,
and all that once laid increase into her womb.
I stood on the hydroelectric dam,
atop the concrete spillway.
I felt the machine-drone
of the deep turbines underneath
trying to say something to my foot bones
through my shoes,

something like, 'I am mighty,
look to me.'

But I had already been naked in rivers
and crossed land over ice lakes in winter,
and been baptized in creeks,
and the dam could not say enough
to convince me, for I knew the mightiness
belonged to open water.

How could a dam endear me to its metal heart?
for when I looked behind me, all the water
was held up now, as though by robbers,
in not a lake, for it had not trees,
nor fauna grown up in the water,
nor flowering wands anywhere near,
nor fish in hundred-year-old holes,
but just a huge holding-tank of still water only.

How could a dam endear me to its metal heart?
for it had made the river
no longer churn properly,
no longer throwing itself into the air with joy,
no longer eddying.
And when I listened, there were wrong notes and
more so, missing notes, to the sound of water there.
The color of the water was not right, too cloudy-eyed
as with a fever, and the smell,
the right smell in the air was missing
at this endless asphalt cistern.

I learnt at the dam about building things
over wild things,
about holding wild things back,
and I learnt from the dam

how to never speak ebullience
but rather only on occasion, sometimes letting out,
yet only in the smallest measured ways,
and always over a controlled spillway...
just some little tiny bit
of something,
but never passion, never vanguard words.

And thus at the dam, I could see
it was meant to teach to hold the tongue,
and to wait and wait
till the gates were opened just a hair,
and only by authority's say so,
and then just to let a modicum
of the most precious through,
leaving behind all the rest of the real water
and her children,
to rage or writhe or wither.

III
Looking for the Headwaters of the Amazon,
I once followed Judy Creek in my 7th winter,
tracking the white rabbits that held
their four-footed dances on the ice.
I did not find.
In the next summer, at the polliwog-glutted,
too-warm-water lagoon,
we were warned away
for the polio lay in wait for children there. ...
I did not find.
Next, I followed the creek at Tower Hill
slogging up the calf-deep water,
stepping over kidlette forts and
babyhand castles on sand bars,

looking, looking for the Headwaters of the Amazon,
but never being able to walk far enough past sunset
for fear to be destroyed by parents' words.

The following summer was the back creek at Rocky Gap.
I did not find.
Then, it was Indiana Dunes, through the clay breaks.
I did not find.
Next, the south bend of the dark green St. Joe river
in French and Indian territory,
still believing like a child Catholic
that 'round the next corner I would find
the Headwaters of Planet Earth,
that raw place where Waterman lived.
But, I did not find.
So ended The Quest for Place Where Water
First Came Out of Earth.

Fifteen years passed, time enough to build
the sense and recklessness
required of a young adventuress,
and I finally stood
at the real headwaters of the real Amazon,
seeing for the first time where water
was first created as Water
that leapt so far into the sky
and then threw itself down on rocks and land
so hard, that as it fell to earth
rainbow after rainbow
was forced from its silver body,
falling and falling into the river
becoming the colors
of lovers in the river,
the lovers in 'the River beneath the river ...'
The Headwaters, indeed.

IV
When I was twenty,
I walked the dry archlands, now underwater.
My cry was too small it seemed, 'No!
you are not burying "ruins."
You are flooding an ancient talking theatre …
one whose voices in juts of rock
will no longer speak over the roar of engines,
nor when its many mouths are drowned with water.'
My grandmother, Querida,
held that the Apocalypse meant not destruction
by fire, rain and flood,
but a return to the senses by sudden quakes
of consciousness, and flooding of memory
that would cause the beauty
and the balance of the land to be restored.
When I wept to her about the river dammed,
the canyons flooded, she closed her milky eye,
and her long white hair rippled
like water cascading, and the roses on her dress
turned into happy fishes …
and she murmured to me
that some see the ancient land as old buildings
to be torn down, and paved over,
but that someday the dam itself
would be seen the same way,
as an old building past its time,
and then, it would be paved over
by the river.

V
When I was in middle age,
I learnt from the water coursing,
real lovemaking,
not the fake kind
they sell in plastic pictures.

I walked miles
up the Cache la Poudre,
climbing over tree lairs,
boulders half in water,
half not.
There I saw and learnt to imitate
how the river loved
every rock frill and ledge,
that the water would lave as high up,
as low down,
as water could reach ...
and how it ruffled up patient,
next urgent, growing in mass
till completely swollen,
then rushing in with
a long smooth hand
along the flanks of the nether banks,
and there the water lingered and eddied,
here and here and here
with a slow back and forth,
lifting back lace from stones,
all hollows and openings finally found.
Downriver water does not only rush
but snaps its hips
and slaps and claps in joyous noise
finally spilling its all everything
over the precipice ... freeing everything
that needs freeing,
filling everything that needs filling.

And after that long thrall,
you can see with your own eyes,
the sudden smooth withdrawal,
the coursing into quiet pools
just the thing ...
that long rest of lovers

in spangled water,
in the place where the soul
ever remembers
herself,
himself,
in the River beneath the river.

VI
The dam tried to capture me,
contain me,
like it once restrained
the mighty river ...
but it cannot have me,
for it was on *el rio abajo el rio*,
the River beneath the river,
that I learned to be wild,
that I learned to make love.

# Death and Decay in the Poudre

## Todd Simmons

*Todd Simmons lived in a yurt at the mouth of Poudre Canyon when he wrote this essay. He publishes and edits the literary and art journal,* Matter, *and runs the Matter Bookstore in downtown Fort Collins. The piece is a mixture of fact and fiction, wistful romanticism and nomadic thinking, and reminds us of the sacredness of bears. Rivers, which are the lifeblood of our continent, have been ravaged beyond comprehension, and in this piece, Todd shows how addressing violence through mythological means is one way of understanding our progress as a species.*

I know a place near the Poudre River where there is a dead and decaying black bear. A few miles past Ted's Place, just before entering the mouth of Poudre Canyon, a bear lies curled up in a dry streambed, wrapped in a fold of the rising foothills. The bear's body lies close to the proposed Glade Reservoir, and every time I visit I think surely the dead bear is a sign of what could happen to the Poudre River.

I'm attracted to rivers that flow freely, that sustain life, to rivers devoid of dams and diversions. I don't *use* rivers like most—I'm not a kayaker, not much of a fisherman, even less the river rat. I like rivers to look at, to drink from, to swim in, to think about descending. My sensibilities do not lend themselves to comfortable days drinking and floating on an inner-tube. My main concern is thinking like a river, because as Jim Harrison says: "Moving water is always in the present tense, a condition we rather achingly avoid." I think a great deal about the health of the Poudre River, visit this decaying bear, and ride the earth like any other human.

I've visited this bear half-a-dozen times already and have every intention of continuing to do so. I revisit every few weeks, watching the rot. In this arid country, decomposition is slow. The lack of precipitation means the decaying black bear will linger for months to come, the hide baking in the hot summer sun, the bones bleached shock-white against the shimmering sage and rabbit brush. I approach this bear with humility and few expectations, trying to attach little significance to this potent symbol of fearlessness and wildness.

The smell of water is often a mixture of the land and attendant creatures living and dying where the water winds down. The Poudre River has a subtle aroma made of equal parts ponderosa pine, sage, and trout—as well as automobiles, summer barbecues, and the occasional forest fire. If you hike away from the Poudre and up toward the bear, its smell would reach you, depending on the course of the wind, a hundred yards before you see it, and immediately you would look for death. A slimy stretch of lime green effluent traces down from the bear's midsection, covering the land ten feet below the body. The entire bear is deflated, almost crushed, half of the lower jaw jutting out without fur or skin. The right shoulder is also bare of fur, the light brown skin covering muscle and ligament and bone. A friend found the bear last summer, and to this day it is remarkable how *intact* the body still is. Although the body remains, the spark of life is gone, transformed into something else. The brute fact that we all die, however, reminds me to look at the bear differently. We all die and go back to the earth—can we ever know the weight and simplicity of this? Death happens every moment, just like that—another body motionless as the hands of time play taps on its lips. It's all over now.

This death-and-decay-watching makes me want to live ever more vividly. I cannot help but both laugh and cry about seeing this bear decompose, rejoining the elements from which it was created. It shakes my conjoined parts all at once, threatening to dismantle my core beliefs.

Pondering all this death, and the potential for more death, causes me to sit up half the night. I pace my yurt and throw my hands in the air at every turn of my mind. The absurdity of this grave-bound world makes me restless. Life, death, life, death—is there any other way, and if so, would it be better? The clock reads 3:00 A.M. I grab my green duffel bag and head for the door. The bag is large enough for me to crawl inside, but I have a different purpose in mind. Despite the many myths surrounding bears, and how very sacred they are—how much magic they contain, even after death—a terribly beautiful act takes hold of my mind and sends me to the rotting black bear.

In the earliest part of the morning, under a clear, star-lit Colorado sky, I hunch over the bear and unzip the duffel bag. I forgot to bring gloves.

The ear tag is the first thing to go. I rip it out of the bear's ear and put it into my pocket. This seems right and makes me smile. My eyesight gets better as the black tone of the sky lightens. I take one last look at the bear, shimmering in the darkness, and grab its right front leg. I hold my breath and pull up on the foot, the skin and fur tearing from the ground. The shoulder comes loose at the joint and I fall back, holding a bear leg. I put this into the duffel, and move to the rear leg. The idea is to move the entire bear into the bag without going piece by piece. The right rear leg rips off as well, and the stench is far worse than earlier today, the mid-section fully open now and maggots spilling out everywhere. I push these into the bag after the legs, not wanting to miss any part of the bear, attached to maggots or not. I get behind the bear and push it into the open bag. It gets stuck at the neck, and I have to twist the bear's head to get it fully inside. I scrape a few piles of fur and skin and intestines into the bag and almost vomit from the stench. I zip the bag closed and try to hoist it to my shoulder.

Due to the awkward angle of the slope, I have to lie down on the ground to get one of the bag's handles around my shoulder, but after doing so I manage to leverage my way to a standing position on the hill. I'm glad the exposed stomach and piles of intestines are at the top of the bag, and not resting on my back. I've never done anything this raw before in my life, and it makes me question the nature of what many take for granted as sanity. I once made my mother stop during a road trip to look at a bobcat killed by an automobile. The dead bobcat looked peaceful lying in the middle of the road. It was not quite cold to the touch. I couldn't bring myself to move the bobcat over into the woods, the aura of death too much to bear. My mother drove the car away and I railed relentlessly at automobiles, confined in and propelled by what I loathed. I felt as if I had treated death in an improper way, that this act might be going too far—a dead bear in a duffel bag on my back? I pick my way down the hillside, shaking my head. I should never act

on ideas at three in the morning. By now the earth has spun around
enough to let sunlight shine on the top of the mountains on the other
side of the Poudre River. I keep going downhill, the walk much easier
owing to the increasing light.

I reach Highway 14 and look both ways. I imagine it's almost 6:00
A.M. but no cars careen down the canyon. I walk over the pavement,
the bear a burden under which I'm beginning to strain. I work down the
other side of the road, the Poudre coursing along within earshot. I walk
up along the river for another half mile before heading to the shoreline.
I put the bear beside the river, and sit down to catch my breath.

These last few months, death has shaped me more than anything.
With the death of a friend's beloved dog, the death of my roommate's
grandfather, the "plans of progress" to kill the Poudre River, and the
bear rotting, death keeps wrenching me into being attentive and engaged. With this bear act, I ask myself, am I thinking like a river now?
We need more action—that's a river talking, right? Humans need more
symbolic, crazy acts, I tell myself, to counteract the forces continuously
wearing us down. Ask a river: There is always another way. I doubt I
could find one person in a thousand who would admit they want to
kill the Poudre River. There must be other forces at work, and I mean
to put a barricade of magic in their way. I reach into the bag and pull
the bear's head from its neck. I raise the head over mine and lob it
straight into the river.

The head makes a walloping splash and then I toss body parts and
handfuls of maggots and other pieces of bear into the river. I've never
heard of a ritual like this, but I'm sure I'm not the first to imagine that
a dead black bear can add some sort of hoodoo-voodoo protection
against confused progress. But it doesn't *mean* anything, this act. I'm
simply one mass, one body, moving another. The significance is in my
own head, and I know this, but I continue to add the bear to the river,
piece by piece. The violence of this act is not lost on me, though my
anger is directed at my own kind and not the bear.

"I'm sorry, black bear. I'm sorry to treat your body in such a way, but
what say you? Can you work your magic even in death?"

The smell emanating from the dead bear gets the better of me, and
I vomit into the river. My watery vomit mixes with the pieces of float-

ing bear and swirls, transforming in the current, floating downstream out of sight. Parts of the bear sink and the bear's paw gets lodged in a rock below me. I wipe my mouth, empty the rest of the bear into the river, and wash out the maggots and gut slime from inside the duffel. It is done, it is finished. There is a dead and decaying black bear in the Poudre River. What do we take out of the river, and what do we put in? One river connects to the next, opening up into oceans, the earth one large watershed. Put something in the Poudre River, and no matter how irreducible, it will eventually end up on the other side of the world. The remains of all your ancestors course down the Poudre River every day, shouting hoodoos and voodoos at you to wake up. Wake up, and take notice of what is going on.

# PART 2

# A Kind of Vertigo

In this section, the writers and poets reflect on the environs of the Poudre and the surrounding landscape. For these writers, the Poudre's world is mostly a nonhuman place that inspires a deeper look at intrinsic nature—the movement of the water, herons, or dippers along the Poudre's edge, or old moose bones collected on hillsides and cliffs. The storyteller's eye initially focuses not inward, but outward. But after reflection, the study of nature seems to enliven the way we see each other too. As Cynthia Melcher writes in her essay examining dippers, "I need to hear a kind of music that can soothe away the woofer-driven chants of human anger and media-generated doom pounding at my ears from everywhere."

# Herons
## John Calderazzo

*John Calderazzo teaches creative nonfiction writing at Colorado State University. He is the author, most recently, of* Rising Fire: Volcanoes and Our Inner Lives, *a book that looks at the many ways in which volcanoes around the world have affected human culture. After straying away from the genre for more than twenty years, he wrote this poem after seeing herons gather above the Poudre as it rolled beside Watson Lake.*

They might have flown in
from China or the Cretaceous,
they look so odd,
great blue herons wheeling
in twos and threes over the red rock wall
carved by the hissing river.

These ancient birds gather
at dusk in my valley—
six, nine, fourteen inkbrush bodies
in sky ballet. They land
with a great springing of legs
on top of the ridge
then fold themselves
into rigid attention,
looking off at the mountains
until darkness sends me home.

At 2 A.M., winds crash
down from the west.
Trees roar like surf,
the backyard windmill blurs
silver in starlight,
and I think of those birds
blown back a million years
or three thousand miles
across the Great Plains,
the Appalachians,
their pterodactyl wings
ripping over the cold Atlantic,
a fragile alphabet lost at sea.

At dusk,
I return to the river.
Twenty herons stand on top of the ridge.

# Rejecting Fast-Food Fishing: Angling the Upper Cache la Poudre

J. D. Phillips

*J. D. Phillips has been a "professional flyfishing something-or-other" for the past twelve years, though now he describes himself as a hobbyist as well as a graduate student in literature. He fishes the upper Poudre, which is seldom fished, because it is always beautiful, enchanting, and meditative. He notes that he goes to this stretch of the river because it helps him imagine rivers without piles of beer bottles, without eroded banks, without stocked trout, without dams—in other words, "without the reminders of failed human relationships with rivers."*

From its beginnings at Poudre Lake on Trail Ridge Road in Rocky Mountain National Park, north to its confluence with the regulated flows of Joe Wright Creek and the traffic on Highway 14, seventeen miles of the Cache la Poudre River can be reached only by pack trail. Because the trail is one of the lesser-traveled routes in the park and because a person can't drive it, the river here gets very little attention from anglers. I've been regularly fishing this stretch between La Poudre Pass Creek and Highway 14 for a few years now, and I have never met another fisherman on the trail. Of course, I'm not complaining. When it seems that much of the West is being overrun in such a short amount of time by leisure-seekers—myself included—I remain hopeful that there will always be rivers and creeks, or pieces of them anyway, that will be overlooked in the rush.

In the evenings at home I spend many late hours running a pencil along the gray contour lines of topographical maps, asking questions of the shaded colors, the dotted and dashed trails and roads, and the curvy blue rivers and creeks: Is there a ridge between the road and stream that would appear impassable to the average automobile-umbilicaled angler?

What's the rating of the trail near that section of stream? Does the river carve the bottom of a narrow canyon? Wait. Look!—a sixty-year-old fire road that's marked abandoned. If any remnants of the road are still there, I could hike it for three miles, turn off into what looks like a meadow, and hmmm …

That's how I became interested in the upper Poudre. When I first arrived in Fort Collins, I traced the entire river on a map from the high plains southeast of town up the canyon and into Rocky Mountain National Park. The first seventeen miles of the river piqued my curiosity, but that's not the first place I fished. For a few months, I joined the summer crowds on the main river along Highway 14, but I was increasingly tired of the lack of etiquette among anglers, the radios blaring in the parking lots, the guides who'd plant their brand-new-everything bedecked clients less than a cast from where I was standing—and also the garbage. Even on *fly only* water, where some claim to be environmentally sensitive, I still found nests of fishing line, fast-food cups and sacks, firerings, and scattered beer bottles—too many reminders of the way western rivers are treated as a convenient way to pass time. The upper Poudre, on the other hand, looked different on the map, and so I was drawn to it because there was no road drawn beside it.

———

On my first attempt to reach the upper Poudre, as I drove up the canyon in late July, I stopped to see pale-morning duns hatching strong and grasshoppers just beginning to be of some interest to trout. I had studied the map the night before, and I could see that to get away from the crowds, I would have to hike five miles from the highway. But I then noticed a winding gravel service road on the map, and I thought if I drove it as far as I could, hiked around a small reservoir and dam that sat on a nearby creek, and then down to where that creek met the upper Poudre, I'd end up in exactly the same place. There was a steep ravine below that dam before it met the Poudre, but the ravine should deposit me in the middle of a nine-mile stretch of the Poudre River with no vehicle access for miles. So with shaky hands I stuffed my rucksack with the necessary supplies and tried to get a decent night's rest.

Turning off the main canyon the next morning, I found the roads I was looking for without too much difficulty. The service road on the map was marked as "maintained," but that wasn't exactly the case. When rocks—submerged like icebergs in the gravel—became too difficult to straddle with the tires and oil pan, I parked the truck, swung my pack around my shoulders, grabbed the fly rod, and headed off on foot. The reservoir was only a short distance farther, and soon I walked along the edge of the water to the near side of the dam. As I walked, I picked up a red wigglers styrofoam carton, some fishing line, and a satin-blue bowling league jacket from somewhere in Kansas. The amount of garbage lying around made me wonder if my new *secret* access to the upper Poudre had already been discovered. With contempt, I placed all the garbage in a neat pile so I could pack it out when I returned to the truck.

I climbed to the top of the dam and looked over the other side. As I expected from studying the map, the ravine did look pretty darn steep, but tall pines shielded the confluence of the creek and the Poudre below from easy discovery. I sidestepped down from the rim of the dam, and started miniature landslides of granitic soil and gravel. When I reached the bottom, the creek banks were too steep to offer a trail, so I was forced to hop from one boulder to another. For nearly a half-mile through dimly lit and mosquito-choked woods, I jumped, skidded, climbed, tested, and jumped again. The creek was littered with boulders so large it seemed I was descending a staircase built for giants. The creek trickled unseen under bellies of the largest stones. About the time I was beginning to wonder what I'd gotten myself into, the ravine leveled off and opened up, and ahead of me sunlight danced on wavy plumes of grass in a small clearing.

Where lodgepoles gave up the forest floor to aspens, I could hear the distant purlings and low hush of the Poudre where it met with the creek. I walked across the grassy clearing, pausing to examine some matted circles of grass where elk or deer had bedded down the night before. Judging by the size of the depressions, I assumed it must have been elk—two cows. From there I walked toward the edge of the Poudre, just upstream from the confluence. Wind gusts chilled the sweat in my hat brim and swirled downstream, shaking the aspens so that their green leaves shimmered like sequins on a dancing dress. And then I saw the river—a green gem, its upstream reaches stretching south into higher country, into mountains whose peaks were still laden with snow.

As I stood there feeling the warmth of my good fortunes, a cutthroat rose and nosed something off of the surface. I tried to remain as still as possible. The fish didn't immediately return to the rocky streambed, but suspended itself in the current. A few seconds later, it inhaled another morsel I couldn't make out. Ahead of that fish, another trout drifted up to the surface with its pectoral fins extended, a brook trout; its colors were darker but no less camouflaged than the cutthroat. As I stood and watched for several minutes, more trout broke the water's surface in every place sheltered from the brunt of the river's flow. Their noses formed rings that passed over and behind their tails and then subsided into the riffles and wavelets of the water. At times, the rises were soft; other times they were splashy and reckless, loud enough to hear over water and wind.

I sat down with my feet dangling in the water and laid my fly rod in the grass. Some fish are too easy, and I couldn't bring myself to wreck the scene by dragging a flailing trout through the river. When I let the pack slip off my shoulders behind me, caddis fluttered out of the grass and headed upstream. The sun felt good on my face and arms, and as I scanned the river and watched rising fish, I noticed something else. Hovering in the air over the water were thousands of olive-bodied mayflies with off-color wings and long tails. Some zipped and darted, but most stayed in one place, bobbing up and down as though hanging from invisible threads. From somewhere in the trees along the river, a wren's song dipped and dove through the muffling sounds of rushing wind. South and upstream, where a dead lodgepole rested on a boulder and leaned at a steep angle over the river, swallows shot through the air, making quick arcs and turns, chasing insects. Above them, perhaps even higher than the treeline on the Mummy Range and the Never Summers, a bald eagle drifted slow deliberate circles alone.

Reaching behind for my pack, I opened it and removed a fly box. Inside I located one of my mayfly concoctions. "A close-enough imitation to do the trick," I thought. I strung the leader and fly line through the guides on the rod and took extra time to knot the fly to the tippet.

I sat in the grass a few more minutes; I wasn't in too much of a hurry. Mayflies performed their dancing flight, the wind spun leaves through the air, and trout splashed after their breakfasts. I sat entranced by the play of water, light, and sound. Deciding that it was still too soon, I stuck the fly into the fly rod cork and laid it back down in the grass. I leaned back on my pack and continued to watch and listen.

Minutes passed undetected and soon became hours, and hours turned into a late morning and an afternoon. I sat there perfectly contented, and never did wet my fly. When the sun dipped below a stand of tall pines and I felt the first chill of the shade, I struggled to free myself from the river's hypnotic embrace. Awkwardly, I stood up, stretched, and took down my fly rod. I loaded the reel into my pack, and took my last few sips of water.

The wind slowed to occasional gusts that rushed through the trees and then died away immediately, leaving only the sound of cracking limbs and falling pinecones. As the wind quieted, the sound of rushing water grew in intensity to fill the voids created by the vanishing light. I started walking back to the ravine and toward my long climb to the reservoir, figuring I had enough day left to make it back safely. My first few steps were clumsy from sitting so long, and I felt drunk with wonder and quiet. To regain some balance, I decided to stand a bit, and so I turned back to the river. The fish had settled down to deeper water when the sun's rays ceased to warm the broken surface. The mayflies had all disappeared too, and only a few caddis fluttered here and there, skittering their abdomens across the water.

A few minutes more, and I continued walking back to the car. As I walked, I realized the map had revealed itself—I had found what I was looking for. This was a magical place, a river lost to those who leave garbage behind, lost to those who treat rivers the way they interact with a fast-food operation. For me, rivers have always given themselves to slow reflection, to be appreciated and known through patience and solitude. Sometimes a river can draw you in to itself, cause you to forget about your wristwatch and any waiting obligations, perhaps even the fly rod in your hand. As I began to climb the first of many boulders stacked in the creek bed, I chuckled to myself, "Next time, I'll try the fishing."

# Poudre Poems
## Robert King

*Colorado-born Robert King has published poems in literary magazines, including* Poetry, Missouri Review, *and* The Atlantic Review, *and in chapbooks, the most recent being* What It Was Like. *He currently teaches part-time at the University of Northern Colorado and has a cabin on the upper Poudre. In these two poems, he explores the moments when the tremendous and delicate influence of "the other" seems to penetrate inwardly—and awaken echoes.*

I.
These nights, the moonlight
edges down the hill's snowy road,
then back up, returning
along a kind of journey.

II.
Reaching the mountain stream this hot day,
I bring both hands full up to my face,
surprised at tasting my own sweat.

III.
The wind, they said,
has the sound
of ten thousand pipes
but tonight
I count only a hundred.

IV.
It's moonlight
that casts the shadow
of this pine
on the snowy road

but it seems like the pine
casting its shadow,
it seems like the snow
receiving the shadow,
nothing to do with moon.

V.
On winter nights
the highway is dark,
the river a long white road.


**Morning in the Long Valley**

Earth holds its breath.
Nothing moves in the crags
above the long valley

nor in the valley itself.
Every pine
doesn't move. And the rocks

move not one small pebble.
Why does this seem
surprising for so long?

Oh, the water would move,
if some were here.
And wind, if it arose,

and the sunlight tumbles
through exact miles
although invisibly.

Still, each thing here stands still.
I start to leave
and nothing notices.

# The Decomposition of Bone Woman

### Deborah Dimon

*Deborah Dimon teaches in the English Department at Colorado State University. She often writes about her experiences in the Cache la Poudre watershed where she has worked in various jobs over the past two decades. In her essay, Deborah reflects on one of the people she met during her seasonal ranger work in the Roosevelt National Forest. The Poudre and its environs shelter all sorts of wonderful critters— human and nonhuman alike.*

There is a man who brings me bones. During the warm months he inhabits the coolness of the Never Summer Range. He lives more than one hundred miles in any direction from the nearest stoplight. He lives at the edge of loneliness, liking it there. His world has no borders. His world is the sagebrush of the mountains, the ryegrasses of the prairie, the yuccas of the desert. He needs to be away, apart. He is homeless. He lives with no mailbox, no schedules, no phones, no one. I do not know where he sleeps in winter.

———

My job takes me to the trails in the Cache la Poudre Canyon and the high country of northern Colorado. These trails are rivers of hooves and paws and feet that follow the path of least resistance. I eagerly retrace their steps, hiking the vegetationless line that unwittingly separates the earth into broad areas, estranging north from south, east from west. I listen for the wind in the lodgepole pines, the thundering falls from the Big South, and the unique colloquial call of the white-crowned sparrow. These sounds pull me deeper into the forest. This rhapsody is in a major key underscoring the gleam of new growth, the drip of melting snows, the return of familiar friends. I set out to explore uncharted places. I find time curled tightly in the frond of a new fern. I recognize that I make random choices with each glance, yet I watch for the patterns and boundaries to emerge. The trail divides. I cannot resist the curving path. It leads to a meadow where there are fresh tracks. It is elk.

I can't say that I clearly remember him, or all of the details surrounding the first time I met the man who brings me bones. But, I do recall the conversation and that I was putting up maps in the Orienteering Room at Arrowhead Lodge Visitor Center. Arrowhead is my canyon headquarters. I work seasonally for the Forest Service as a Natural and Cultural Resource Interpreter. He had also worked for the Forest Service once, somewhere in Wyoming. He liked the USFS taking old Arrowhead Lodge, and using it as a visitor center, to educate the public about Poudre Canyon and Roosevelt National Forest. He liked the programs, books, maps, and displays. He liked that an already developed site was being put to use. And so he asked, "Could you use some relics I found?"

On a Sunday, several weeks later when I got to the lodge in the morning, a plastic bag with my name on it hung from the rusted Coke-bottle-door-handle on the front porch. It contained an assortment of moose and bird bones. Each specimen was tagged and identified, but no one had signed the note, and I didn't remember his name. I put the bones in the display case next to the bighorn sheep hooves.

As I was locking up for the evening, the seductive smell of sage intruded upon my task and lured me to linger on the porch. The canyon was silent. After hours, the window panes of Arrowhead are black and conceal the inner emptiness, reflecting only the outer world. Secretive and somnolent, the chalky fingers of the surrounding aspens stretch to touch bruised clouds. This time of year, late spring, the hillsides covered with rabbit brush resemble mangy coyotes about to lose their winter fur. The bighorns are moving up. The elk have already grazed through. The return of the broad-tailed hummingbirds is celebrated. The air is moist. A brown van stops in the driveway. It is the man who brings me bones. I recognize his face.

As I approach the van he throws his head back, alarmed. His nostrils flare, eyes open wide, he tenses, alert, like a riderless horse that needs to know what I am before he'll allow me to get close. He recognizes me as the USFS interpreter and relaxes. The sun is warm and tender on my back in the cool evening air. I shiver as he rolls down his window.

He is a confident man, with a genuine smile. His face is weathered and browned and his eyes are startlingly blue. A topaz blue. He gets out of the van and we walk over to the porch steps to sit and talk. He walks like a cowboy, knees cocked. He wears a plaid flannel shirt that looks soft and clean, as if he hangs his shirts on a line to be dried in the sun. His muscles are sinewy. His sandy-colored hair is short and just beginning to recede. He settles on his heels, squatting comfortably in front of me at the bottom of the porch steps.

As we talk he draws circles on the ground with a stick stirring an imaginary campfire. He tells me he feels clumsy with words, but I think he is articulate and certainly knowledgeable relating a tale about tracking a mountain lion in the Narrows that was simultaneously tracking him. He notes the lion's infinite patience. He reveals the steps of the kill, one by one, like dropped bread crumbs ... the sudden flash of tan in the rocks above him. No sound. Each aware of the other's presence. Circling. The elusive figure padding between shadows, slipping in and out of the bright meadow at the fringe of deep trees; the stiff doe, half-buried under brush; her punctured neck, the dried blood. He tells me he documents it as a confirmed sighting. Even the secretive mountain lion, he concludes, leaves a trace in the wilderness.

I tell him I know many locals, people who have lived and worked here all of their lives, who have never seen a mountain lion. My husband has keen eyes and keeps track of a long list of animals he has sighted in the thirty years he has lived here. Remarkably, he has never seen a mountain lion. As I talk with the man who brings me bones, we decide that seeing animals, especially reclusive cougars, is like counting coups.

He tells me that names are important, and that he creates personal, secret, descriptive names for places that are special to him. He looks me in the eyes and says that revealing the personal name of a place to someone who will not honor it, exposes it and takes away the powers that make that place wondrous. Caring about these places, giving them names that capture their character, their nature, is a way to protect the magic, he says. I understand. He wants me to steer people away from the still "undiscovered" places in the area. He wishes I would simply direct a visitor to Poudre Falls, but not reveal or mention the "Guardian of the Falls" whose vigilant eyes mysteriously peer into the lacy froth. He whispers, "The magic must be protected." He points out that Native Americans acknowledged the mystical powers of remarkable places, events, and people through their names. I nod. I tell him I will call him "The Man Who Brings Me Bones." He laughs.

We talk comfortably together, as if we are old friends, picking up where we left off. Another life? He is in no hurry. I know my family is waiting, hungry, but I relax, listening to the cadence of his voice, trying to think of who he reminds me of ... no one, I decide. When I tell him I should go home, that my family is waiting, he quietly says that his cousin is his family. He got a letter from her. He stands up.

I think he is leaving, heading for his van without saying good-by. But his voice reaches me in mid-sentence as he walks back from his van, letter in hand. His cousin is a botanist in North Dakota. She knows the names and nuances of the prairie grasses. He sits down next to me, carefully pulling the letter out of the envelope. Her printing is the smallest I have ever seen, as if she doesn't want her words to be seen. The Man Who Brings Me Bones tells me his cousin shares his day of birth. She was in a terrible car accident when she was a young girl. It disfigured her face and both of her parents died in the crash. A drunk driver. I hear in the gentleness of his voice that he loves her heart. He tells me how beautiful she is. He worries aloud that she may never know the love of a man. She is a researcher, she knows the land, the plants. He begins reading her letter, slowly, savoring the contact:

> Montana, 199–
> Dear Cousin,
>     ... Montana is everything you told me it would be. The Park
> I visited is named in honor of Chief Plenty Coups. His story was
> originally translated by an old trapper named Linderman, based
> on Plenty Coups' reminiscences. He was a Crow chief troubled by
> the encroachment of the whites upon his land, his people, he did
> not know how to lead his people through these troubling times in

*a land he no longer recognized. Tired and hot from his wander-*
*ings in the relentless sun of the prairie, he sat down to rest in the*
*shade of a lone tree. Not knowing what to do to help his people,*
*he despaired, head in hands. Then, an apparition appeared to*
*him in the form of a Man-person, an annunciation. The Man-*
*person shook a red rattle and sang an odd song. "Look!" he said,*
*then disappeared. In the Man-person's place was a dark forest. A*
*fierce storm came. The sky was black. The four winds brutalized*
*the forest. The chief's heart was scorched with pity. After the*
*storm passed there was only one tree standing where once the for-*
*est had been. This spared tree is the lodge of the Chickadee. He is*
*tiny, the voice said, but has the strongest mind among all birds.*
*He never misses an opportunity to learn from others. The lodges*
*of many Bird-people were in that forest when the Four Winds de-*
*stroyed it. One solitary lodge is left unharmed, the lodge of the*
*Chickadee-person. Learn from the Chickadee, Plenty Coups. Do*
*not despair.*

The Man Who Brings Me Bones looks up to see if I am following
the story, to see if I care. I nod and he reads on.

> *…I have found peace among the native grasses. Plenty*
> *Coups' spirit is everywhere. I came here to sort through some*
> *things. You know how it is, I found myself sitting on a bench in*
> *the welcome shade of a lone tree here in the grassland, head in*
> *hands, my usual despair. How can I go on? Plenty Coups then*
> *rattled me. He came to me as a vision and a voice. Chick a dee*
> *dee dee dee dee dee. Chick a dee dee dee dee dee dee.*
>
> *Love,*
> *Your favorite cousin*

I feel him studying me, a species he is examining for habits. The
scrutiny makes me feel like a trapped bird, the size of a chickadee. I am
cupped in his hands. My heart beats wildly. I think about the irony of
delicate birds descending from dinosaurs. I am being crushed. With my

conversation, I seize the opportunity and escape, flying toward the clouds, out of reach. My chest expands. Breathing, breathing. Lifting my shoulders, I inhale deeply. The silence has form. I exhale, uncomfortable with the pulse of this moment and rein away from the attraction.

Intimacy slithers along the ground, a guilty evening shadow. I straighten my badge and fidget with the clasp. He seems to have some understanding of me that I don't know how to accept or describe. He carefully re-folds the letter, sliding it back into its envelope. He slips it into a Zip-loc for safekeeping. The staccato snap of the baggie ribs being pinched together punctuates the distance I am wedging between us.

He gently changes the direction of the conversation, sensing my withdrawal. He tells me the moose bones he left for me at Arrowhead were found near Glendevey, north of Stub Creek in the Laramie River Valley last year. The moose wallow in the willows close to where he parks his van to hike the Rawahs. I tell him a moose was spotted from the laundry room at Glen Echo Resort last week—quite low for moose, a gold mine for the owners of the resort. I thank him for the treasures he left for the displays. He is pleased that the bones have found a home where they can help educate visitors and children. "Have you ever seen a moose toe?" he asks. The preposterous question makes me smile.

As we talk, the layers of mountains turn from violet to deep indigo. It's almost dark, late, but the conversation is light and frivolous. I ask him why he chose to live in the Poudre. He says he ran out of places he wanted to go. He tells me he lives in his van, lives on rubber wheels. He's a Michelin Man. We laugh easily together. Like the elk, he moves to the high country in the summer, lower turf in winter. I think of the fervent migration of the mergansers, winging their way to mate and nest in the higher pools along the river as the days warm. This man will always migrate alone.

As night weighs in, the mighty mountains of the canyon are now shapes, no longer layered. They are black delineating blue. The mountains in the distance crowned with lingering snow are sapphires. I want more conversation, but there is nothing more that can be said this evening. I signify closure, asking if he will be bringing me any more bones. I am surprised at myself, for I don't listen for his reply, but am wondering what it would be like to be in this man's arms? Weightless,

I think. But I cannot allow myself the luxury of defying gravity. My family is waiting. I race to the underbrush.

————

Sometimes I forget why I am married. It is easy as years pass to dwell on what is not, rather than appreciate what is. Sometimes I have to stop and review my memories, assess my emotions. I recognize different kinds of love, the interludes that surge and ebb like the river. I respect a man who is steady. Feet firmly on the ground, rooted, secure and safe. A man who knows the meaning of a day's work, a dollar, a home, a family. He is gentle, he is kind. Once, when the swallows nesting on our porch were losing patience trying to entice their young to leave the nest and fly, he reached into the birdhouse and pulled out one of the fledglings. Cradled in his two great hands he gently tossed it into the air. It awkwardly flew a few feet, then fell to the ground. He picked it up and placed it back in the nest. An hour later, the birdhouse was empty. They were all flying.

Sometimes I wish I had worn a real wedding gown when we were married. Yards of ivory organdy, with a long train, like curtains fluttering at the window. The kind of gossamer gown that is put into a cedar trunk to be saved for the children's children, but is never worn again. The kind that is shrouded in a dry cleaning bag, saved from calcifying in the light. My wedding dress was a serviceable white blouse with lace trim and a denim skirt. Practical. They hang together in the closet, next to my spare uniform, waiting for an occasion. I have to be careful though—sometimes the lace catches on my badge.

I read an Indian legend in one of the books at Arrowhead. It is a story belonging to an ancient tribe of the Southwest—"La Huesera," the story of the Bone Woman. Her work is collecting bones and preserving that which is in danger of being lost to the world. She inhabits a cave filled with the skeletal remains of deer, crows, rattlesnakes, and wolves. She explores the mountains, the draws, and dry riverbeds searching for bones. Her goal: to reassemble an entire carcass. When the perfect skeleton is completed she sings to it. As she raises her voice, the indestructible framework of life—the bones—defiantly rise up. The sculpture becomes a creature that breathes, laughs, and races down the canyon. Somewhere in the running—it may be from the speed, or splashing through the river, or perhaps the catalyst is a ray of the sun—the creature transforms into a laughing woman who runs wild and free to the canyon ridge. It is said that if you are lost or weary, La Huesera may visit you and show you the flesh of the soul.

Sometimes I think I would like to have her powers, and other times I would rather be the bones. Found, retrieved, reassembled. A chance at a new life. This time wild. This time untamed.

————

As the spring rolls into summer, I start spending a lot of time working with John Slay, the Forest Service archaeologist. He is about to retire, but neither his pace nor his enthusiasm are waning. He gives me a crash course on the ancient sites excavated in the area. His enthusiasm is catching. He knows all the archaeological locations in the Arapaho-Roosevelt National Forest. He shows me the documentation on the tipi rings in the big meadow near the "Welcome Home" fence. It was Slay who told me about the significant find at what I call Catkins Creek. I can't wait to share this find with my friend. It has been weeks since I last spoke to The Man Who Brings Me Bones, but I have seen him taking photos of bighorns in the Narrows, and I know he hiked the far side of the river at Dutch George Flats. I saw his van parked at the Dips.

As I drive up the canyon one day in midsummer, I see him below Hombres, binoculars trained on a pair of golden eagles playfully circling each other over the crags of Gunsight Peak. I pull over. I see him take out a small notebook and pencil from his shirt pocket to record their maneuvers. I want to tell him about the Catkins Creek site that is east of Stove Prairie Landing, north of the Devil's Backbone, west of Greyrock, and just south of Phantom Canyon. I want to tell him about the discovery there, but my husband and I are expecting relatives, and I have to get the groceries home and dinner started. I'm running late, and though we speak for a bit, I dash off before I say a word about it.

A few days later, I put on long pants and tall boots. I drive down the canyon. I set out walking for the Catkins Creek site in the cool morning. Yucca and prickly pear cactus stand guard at the trailhead. By 9 A.M. it is already hot. I think about the records and maps Slay showed me regarding the discovery of the ancient bones. In 1963, a trace of gray showed up, evidence of organic material, leaching out among the layers of ochre clay along the banks of the creek—the smudge betrayed the location. A USFS archaeologist interpreted the sign and soon unearthed the bones of a Paleo-Indian woman. The archaeologist was surprised by both the gender and the era, and was startled to see that her bones were red, painted red. Why?

As I walk along, the site is farther than I thought. The temperature continues to rise. I stop for a drink of water. She haunts me. I see myself as her dead spirit returning to dance on the thirsting seeds, the seeds germinating in the dark, on the ground that her decaying body nourished. The winds rattle the parched grass. I am the dust of the earth and rain. Was she?

Was she exhumed to be painted by her people long after her flesh had decayed? Or worse, was her flesh scraped away from her bones with primitive chert knives while she was still warmly rotting? Did the paint slow the process of decomposition? Did the red color brand her like the wearer of Nathaniel Hawthorne's rubric?

My expedition turns out to be uneventful. No snakes, no spiders, no answers. I'm not even sure I have found the exact site. I hike out to the highway, drive home, and shower the heat and the dust away.

———

Late summer, and for the third morning in a row I have found a plastic bag filled with moss-flecked bones hanging on the front porch at Arrowhead. This time I do not seek a name. As I catalog the bones, I speculate. What will he become? As age replaces vitality, will he become like the guy we call "Cadillac Man" who sits all day in his Cadillac in the Lower Canyon—*Mandible, caudal vertebra, tibia*—who is crazy from loneliness? Will he sit alone in his van day after day watching the river flow, simply growing fat and filthy? Will he be "Van Man"—*Distal end of tibias exhibiting spiral fracturing*—or will he be found ranting about thirty-five acre ranchettes and those who can afford them?

*Calcaneum, scapula, femur.* Will he publish the detailed journal he keeps with the photos he takes, becoming a legendary naturalist, famous for his eccentricities? *Thoracic vertebrae, ribs, lumbar vertebrae.* Will he declare in a too-loud voice to any animal that will listen that the flash of tan in the pine was not a mountain lion at all, but the golden eyes of a coyote? *Ulna, humerus, otolith.* "A coyote so close you could see the black storm in the pupils." I put the bones away on the top shelf of the cupboard in my office for safekeeping until I decide exactly how to arrange them for the new display.

One night after cataloging the bones, I dream: It is a no-moon night, and I am standing on the front porch at Arrowhead Lodge peering into the darkness. I'll need a flashlight, but it is my voice I have lost, and even in the dream I know a flashlight will not help. There is someone else standing on the porch. I know instinctively it is him, The Man Who Brings Me Bones. He knows why I am peering from the porch, mute. I hear a heart pounding, hooves on the plains. I exhale, exasperated with my silence. I expect the cycles of the earth to whisper their secret in my ear. They do not. I only see stars.

My husband is in the dream, too, close enough to whisper in my ear, but he remains silent. The skeletons of animal stars are pulsing, magnified. I forget if I'm looking at stars or fainting. Then there it is, my voice, falling from Ursa Major, the great bear, searing the sky. I open my mouth and my voice lands on my tongue, a sizzling communion. The Man Who Brings Me Bones asks me a question I do not fully understand, but I answer him anyway. "It is safe here, though the world is decomposing. This is a good thing. From decay comes new life; it is as it should be."

———

In November, I hike the Winterstein, south of the Lady Moon Ranch, just above the sawmill. The smell of smoke from a nearby hunter's camp is in the air. White ash lands on the cedars and on my shoulders like tiny white moths. The season is over and so is my job. A time for letting go. Even the name of this season, *autumn,* is mournful and minor. I hear the *teep…teep* of a Townsend's Solitaire in the distance. It reminds me of a haiku that recognizes that we always long for something even if we already possess it—longing to be in Kyoto, while in Kyoto.

Just off the trail is something white and large. An elk carcass. It is missing a leg—no, two legs, and silently grinning at the sky. The skeleton is picked clean, no sign of a hide. No sign of crows. Still attached are both back teeth the size of hominy, like two tiny ivory tusks. A testimony to evolution. I kick at the teeth. I kick again, harder this time. *Crunch*, again*, crunch*. The ivory rips away from the jaw. The carcass gawks toothlessly. This is the kind of gift The Man Who Brings Me Bones would appreciate and accept. I could give him one tooth and keep the other one for myself, like friendship medallions. I put the ivory in a plastic bag.

———

In the canyon, winter is the color of a sparrow. The river is not blue at all, but black. The sun is a lone elk grazing into the long night. I am toasty, lying in bed with a good book of poetry and a cup of chamomile. The temperature outside drops. I wonder where The Man Who Brings Me Bones is. I have not seen him in two months. He once told me that giving and receiving warmth is the skeleton of our existence. It is what makes us human. His thin bones must crave warmth. I put my book down, no longer interested in extravagant words. I worry that spring will find him dead, too late for a coffin. "Good thing," he'd say, "to become earth's soup."

# First Night Without Rain
Steve Miles

*Steve Miles is a high school teacher and lives in Denver with his wife, Teri, and kids, but makes frequent pilgrimages back to the Poudre and friends up north. His most recent publication is in* Comeback Wolves: Western Writers Welcome the Wolf Home. *One evening, after rain, he came to the river's edge, and was startled by the clarity of the moon and the stampeding power of the river. As he notes, "The river had a different personality now, one that commanded respect in a more dangerous way. My watching became a kind of vertigo."*


The moon
looks freshly bathed.

The Cache la Poudre River
     is a silvery slush of sibilance
roughly shouldering
the high bank.

Where we made love
is underwater.

Fireflies hover
there.  The mare,
suddenly stirred,
gallops a wide
half-circle
with her foal
& is gone.

If she rises
much more
the fire-ring
will wash.

A milkweed blossom
lifts from its stem
& flutters off.

Only the fox
knows just
where I am.

I turn
at a sound
licking
the dewy grass.

Under the pile
of broken crates
the lid
of a single eye
rises.

# Desperate for River Refugia

Cynthia Melcher

*Having inhabited many regions of the United States, Cynthia Melcher has found a sense of place in deserts, mountains, coastal places, woodlands, and grasslands, but she has always found her greatest sense of solace in the voices of birds. After moving to Colorado to study the declining population of white-tailed ptarmigan in Rocky Mountain National Park and begin a career in avian conservation research, she discovered dippers, canyon wrens, and other songsters of our western river systems. Her essay, "Desperate for River Refugia," results from several brief escapes from the loneliness and hopelessness that came from working long days on conservation plans.*

I'm careening down that turbulent mainstream of living only to work and face standing waves of serial deadlines with their attendant souse holes of isolation while the flood waters become so swollen that most of the quiet eddies are subsumed by the monstrous torrent, and I can't figure out how to stop and get out and restore myself or reach for something my spirit can grab onto so I can escape this exhausting rush ...

I need to hear a kind of music
    that can soothe away the woofer-driven chants
    of human anger and media-generated doom
    pounding at my ears from everywhere;

I crave inhalation of lucid, fragrant air
    to displace the thickening choke
    that blows off production lines
    of human industriousness;

I must have daily contact with life sources
    instead of making do with virtual realities
    and actual episodes of rigor mortis
    setting up like concrete in my soul.

I try to remember
    when the current ran more slowly,
    how easy it was to pull out
    and find refuge on this side of the edge …

I especially treasure a long-ago morning along the Cache la Poudre, where a dipper's song cascaded off the canyon wall at Picnic Rock and stopped me in my tracks. It was March, when ice still bound much of the river, including its shaded southern edge along the wall. As I meandered over the rocks—exposed by the diminished flows of winter—a pair of dippers appeared from the water and hopped onto the shelf of melting ice. One of them proceeded to sing as if to celebrate the imminent equinox, as if to encourage the river into reopening all the way upstream to his nesting territory. That song ran on and on like the river itself, tripping and splattering through riffles of whistles and sharp call notes, then pooling in slow-swirling eddies of soft, low chortles before slipping over the next ledge in a waterfall of trills and misty buzz notes. My ears would have followed his song all the way to the sea.

———————

The American Dipper was named for its odd habit of repeatedly jouncing down-then-up. *Cinclus mexicanus*—the bird's scientific name—derives from the Greek word root, "cincl," which translates as "wagtail." Yet, the dipper does not wag its tail. Rather, the bird crouches, dipping its entire body downward while turning its head this way, then it springs up and back down again while turning its head that way, then bounces back up and down—the tail simply dips with the rest of the bird. No one is certain why dippers do this, but while watching and listening to them that morning at Picnic Rock, I began to believe that they dip to keep the beat:

dip look right *trill trill jigik buzz,*
dip look left *babble trill trill trill,*
dip look right *chortle brzzt trill brzzt,*
dip look left *trill chortle zzeet-zzeet-zzeet*

As I became totally absorbed in their antics, time itself washed downstream, taking with it those distracting surges of adrenaline required to stay afloat while steering every minute of each day around countless obstacles.

Suddenly, the birds plunged back into the river, no doubt to look for another meal. Although the dipper is a mere featherweight, whose body would fit perfectly in my slightly cupped hand, it's a chunky-looking bird with strong, stubby wings and long, gripping toes. It uses these tools to go after prey in clear, cold, rushing mountain waters. With powerful downstrokes, dippers fly through the current to the streambed, where frictional forces slow the water's velocity enough to allow the birds a toehold on the rocks. Underwater, they half-fly-half-hike upstream to poke under pebbles and stones, seizing with their bills aquatic larvae, small fish, or the eggs of fish and amphibians, and then emerging to gulp them down. More than any other songbird on this continent, the dipper—also known as the water ouzel—is utterly at home in its aquatic habitat. And when one of these birds flies from place to place, it does not veer from the river's course. It would sooner fly the extra mile—
leaning
        left

            then

                    right

            then

     left

around each bend—than leave its riverine world.

Finally, the dippers popped up for air, apparently without having staved off their hunger. They floated themselves on the water like ducks, saving energy by letting the river carry them back downstream before resuming their upstream hunt. I don't know how long I watched those little gray sprites that morning as they dipped and rushed about, embodiments of the river itself, but I know they brought me right back to myself. Their gift was something I could not have found in a mall or from outlets of technology, nor could I have earned their gift by logging endless hours at work and doggedly paying the bills.

———

It is now years later, and I'm desperate. The mainstream finally slowed a little this week, although it still took several attempts to break away from work early. Miraculously, I have returned to Picnic Rock. It stormed earlier on this mid-August afternoon, cooling and refreshing the air, but, when I arrive, the rocks at the river's edge are already dry. The daily summer hordes of boats, inner tubes, and "river rats" have also evaporated. Only a couple of fly fishermen remain. I pick a nice, flat-topped boulder and perch—cross-legged—with my journal in my lap. I let my eyes close and listen, hoping to hear little dipper voices rising over the Poudre's late-summer babble.

Moments waft by before the drama being played out by two belted kingfishers snatches my attention. They fly directly over me while adding their maraca-like voices to the symphony of river music, forcing me to open my eyes and wonder what's going on. As if called in by the commotion, a trio of Steller's jays suddenly alights in the broad willow that casually reaches over my rocky perch. They nearly encircle me as they rasp out their calls, apparently hoping I will hand them something to eat. When they realize that I cannot be conned, they move on, and my eyelids close again. From just downstream, I also hear the harsh, down-slurring *peeee-errr* song of a western wood-pewee above the sound of the river. A smile slowly sneaks across my face. What a treat to hear him singing this late into August, when most of the other songbirds have already quit for the season. But somehow the kingfishers, the jays, and even the wood-pewee do not take me to the same place those little spirits of the river took me that late winter morning years ago. I've scanned all the rocks within my view for signs that dippers have been here recently, but I see no whitewash topping on any of them. I finally have to accept that the dippers are not here now. They must have moved upstream, where I imagine them working hard to fill the gaping mouths of recently fledged young.

I sit a while longer, inhaling the vanilla aromas of ponderosa pine and casting my eyes upstream one last time. As my gaze floats along with the current, I fall under the spell of surface ripples as they metamorphose on the rocks underwater into dancing pairs of shadow and light. Eventually, I find myself staring straight down the upstream facet of my perch and into the face of a hefty, two-inch-long insect clinging to the rock just above water level. Its size—and the fact that I only just notice it—jar me out of my reverie.

———

The insect's elongated abdomen is ringed with dark-brown stripes, and a zigzag of brown and white jags across its forehead. The six partially fringed legs protrude outward at various sharp angles and end with two opposing "claws" that hold it to the rock. It sports two pairs of little wing pads, and two long "tails" (cerci) protrude from the end of its abdomen. These characteristics—not to mention the rocky, rushing-river habitat— tell me that this is the nymph of a stonefly, specifically *Claassenia sabulosa*. A mayfly nymph would have just one claw on each leg, and many species of mayfly sport three cerci. I touch it lightly to see what it will do, and immediately realize that "no one is home"—it is only the discarded husk, or "shuck," of a stonefly nymph. Nevertheless, I'm thrilled with this discovery because I know that stoneflies are high on the dipper's menu.

*Claassenia sabulosa* spends the first three years of its life lurking around the protection of large rocks in the river before emerging to molt one last time and begin its brief, aerial life as a reproductive being. Evidently, the one on my perch had emerged recently. Quickly, my eyes leap from rock to rock, and I begin to see stonefly nymphs everywhere—one or more on each emergent rock. Although all of them have been vacated, those claws still grip tightly to the sites where they exited from their watery world. What a mass exodus of wings this must have been. I wonder when and how far upstream it all happened. I can picture dipper families up there, gorging themselves at their tables of river rock, piled with squirming nymphs.

Knowing that their prey are so abundant here at Picnic Rock makes it seem possible that dippers could go on thriving in the Poudre River.

Stoneflies are the canaries of western river systems. If the water sickens with heavy metals, if it warms too much as trees and other shade-bearing plants are cut, munched, or trampled away from its banks, if sewage and fertilizers boost algal blooms that rob it of oxygen, if too much water is diverted away to waste on lawns and water-intensive crops, stoneflies are among the first to succumb. So the remains of stonefly nymphs that surround me are like streaks of hope shining over the coming horizon of winter. I may not have found dippers today, but I have seen what may bring them back here.

––––––––

It's now the end of August, just two weeks after my return to Picnic Rock, and I have grabbed another chance to return to the river. My need to find refuge in the lives and songs of dippers has intensified and compels me farther upstream. I head to the place where a certain bridge crosses the river. For many years, I know that bridge has provided the perfect infrastructure—protected ledges overhanging whitewater—for nesting dippers.

Almost as soon as I reach the water's edge at the bridge, I spot a dipper peering at me from atop a rock just twenty feet away. With its back to me, the chunky little bird dips, looking at me over its left shoulder, then dips and checks me out with its right eye. But the bird disappears when I'm suddenly distracted by someone on the bridge telling me to move my car to the official parking lot downstream. I comply, then return to the river's edge and begin a careful quarter-mile trek upstream—half-terrestrial-half-aquatic—toward the bridge. I pick my way from rock to rock, trying not to slip on slick, dark-green algae that coat the submerged rocks. I find myself wishing for a set of dipper gripping toes or the clingy claws of a stonefly, but I must make do with my techno-Tevas.

Along my route, I spot more stonefly shucks and dipper wash adorning many of the emergent rocks in this reach of river. But about halfway to the bridge, I notice a heavy blanket of silt and sand draped across the riverbed. It does not take long to figure out where it all came from—a gaping culvert that disgorges runoff from the road above into the river. Stonefly nymphs and other dipper prey inhabit the protective crevices between rocks and stones in the river. *Claassenia sabulosa* nymphs, in particular, require large, unembedded rocks in their riverine habitat. There, they can escape the water's powerful turbulence, but if those little refugia become clogged with silt and sand, stoneflies sometimes disappear. I find no stonefly shucks at this spot, and I wonder how many of the Poudre River's macroinvertebrate neighborhoods have already been in-filled this way.

Finally I make it to the bridge. Looking up and looking down the river, jouncing and turning almost dipper-style, I glance about for the bird. Within seconds, my eyes catch sight of a dipper nest under the bridge. The architects of this domed nursery had chosen to build on the eastern base of a steel I-beam that supports the bridge. The nest is probably eight or ten inches in diameter and perfect—a lovely globe of sturdy grasses and leaves interwoven with finer fibers. Facing the morning sun and oriented somewhat south of the nest's equator is the large entrance hole. The nest site—recessed from the bridge's outer edge by several feet—protects it from Colorado's hot afternoons and occasional drenching thunderstorms.

Like almost all dipper nests, this one teeters precariously over whitewater. The I-beam base on which the nest sits appears only as wide as a windowsill. But, with their built-in code to swim and float, dippers would rather nest where they risk their babies to the rushing torrent than to a site that could allow easy access for snakes and other critters inclined to dine on nestling birds. So I wonder about big, blue, rubber rafts bedecked with squealing squads of orange-helmeted anthropoids bristling with long paddles as they slide just inches under the nest. How does the dipper respond to them? I just hope that rafters also have a code—to pass under bridges silently with paddles down so that they do not inadvertently launch young dippers into the water before their time.

As I study the nest under the bridge, I notice two or three big, round stains on the I-beam to either side of the nest ... nest-prints of bigger structures now gone. In fact, as large as this nest is, it does not compare to some of the dipper nests I've discovered in other places. Year after year, dippers may reuse or rebuild on top of their old nests, augmenting them with more material each breeding season until the structures become so bulky and top heavy that they fall into the torrent below. The relative smallness of this nest tells me that it is probably a recent housing start, and I look forward to coming back here in late winter to watch them build their next addition.

As I poke around the bridge for signs of other historical nest sites, I notice dipper tracks in a mini-mudflat on the footing of one bridge abutment—now exposed by the diminished flows of late summer and a wholesale caching of the Poudre's currency into cash-green reservoirs. I work my way over to the tracks and dip down for a look. For a bird that weighs so little, the dipper has made fairly deep tracks. It must have dipped and dipped here, each time pressing its weight deeper into the muck. In one spot, a semicircle of tracks indicates that the bird gradually turned 180 degrees,  as if it kept looking farther over its left shoulder than to the right each time it dipped.

––––––––

But somehow the tracks and nest are just not enough. Where has the dipper gone? I tell myself to be patient, but never before have I known a dipper to be so quiet and elusive. I'm not sure what's up. I settle down to wait a while longer, confident that eventually a dipper will zoom right by me—barely two feet above the water and announcing its arrival with a triple *zzreet*. Meanwhile, I kneel at the river's edge and focus downward, hoping to find more clues about dipper life. Right away, my eyes glom onto countless little tubes, or "caves," apparently made of sand grains somehow glued together. They're clustered in protected crevices and on the downstream facets of the rocks. Looking up to check the rocks exposed due to falling water levels, I see the same phenomena and—peering one-eyed into the open end of a dry sand tube—I begin to understand. These miniature caves are the vacated hideouts of caddisfly nymphs. So here again I see signs of dipper food everywhere, and caddisflies are considered even more delectable than stoneflies! I can't resist wondering whether a dipper would tweeze the caddisfly nymph from its casing, crack the casing open to access the insect inside, or gulp the whole thing down—sand and all. Since most birds have to ingest a certain amount of mineral grit to help their gizzards grind food, perhaps the dippers consume these "caddisfly wraps" as all-in-one-mineral-sup-plemented-meals.

My curiosity prompts me to pick up a stone and scrutinize it. There, a creature not even a half-millimeter long wriggles under the surface tension of water still clinging to the stone. It looks like the first or second instar of a stonefly or mayfly—a perfect miniature of the hulks I've seen over the last two weeks. I also see a cluster of slightly tapered tubes, only a quarter- to half-inch long. They're made of a paper-like substance, are somewhat square in cross section, and have been tethered by one end to the stone. Another species of caddisfly? One that does not prefer to cloak itself in sand? I pluck one of the tubes from its rock, set it down in a tiny pool at the edge of the river, and immediately the occupant's head emerges. It looks like a tiny hermit crab that has been stretched out on a rack. Then at least one pair of legs also emerges and impels the tube up a small stem as the nymph searches for a new anchor.

My attention then wings out over the mainstream, where a thin swarm of yellowish insects bobs only a foot above the water. From this distance, they appear to be small stoneflies or caddisflies, but my human vision is not powerful enough to identify them. Then I see smaller, whitish flies drift upstream to mingle with the crowd. What are they all doing out there, dancing around in the morning sun? Maybe it's a mate-finding performance, or perhaps they're depositing their next generations into the Poudrebank of macroinvertebrate eggs? Either guess bodes well for dipper stocks and futures.

Still, the dipper I saw earlier has not returned. Reaffirming one more time my commitment to stay until it reappears, I unfold from my journal a copy of the *Birds of North America* dipper account, settle down with my back resting against a huge boulder, then begin to read. Not very far into it, I learn of yet another way in which dippers live like ducks. Apparently they molt all their flight feathers at once and undergo up to fourteen days of flightlessness! This discovery astounds me. As a professional ornithologist, why didn't I know that? This tells me that I've grown too comfortable with scientific generalizations. Yes, most songbirds molt only a few flight feathers at a time so they can continue to escape predators and look for food as they renew their wings, but it never occurred to me that dippers might have another strategy. Feeling chagrined, I read on. Also like ducks, dippers seek the relative safety of secluded refugia to wait out their flightless period, which—it turns out—is late August!

Well, OK. I've been utterly *"had."* Those little river sprites I've been seeking all this time must be lurking quietly in a suitable dipper hide-out while they molt and regrow their flight feathers. Whether they have retreated upstream to special molting sites or are watching me right now from under nearby cover, I finally realize that this is not their time to make themselves known. The dipper I saw earlier today must have emerged from hiding only briefly to find food. No wonder I never saw where it flew during that earlier commotion on the bridge. I suppose it just ducked underwater and scuttled to better cover.

Reluctantly, I decide to head for home. I fold the dipper account back into my journal, take one last hopeful look around, then clamber back up the river bank and trek along the road toward my car. Immediately I'm hit with the *whoosh* of heavy traffic and the choke of diesel fumes exploding from megatrucks straining to haul RVs up the canyon. When I finally reach the relative refuge of my car, I reassure myself that if I made it this long, I can wait it out a little while longer until the dippers emerge—like stoneflies—from their safe havens. Coasting downhill, I ease the transition by shifting into a dipper day-dream and leaning way

    left

        then

                right

        then

  left

as I negotiate each bend in the road. Already, my mind is scanning the near future for another chance to pull out, when I can rejoin the dashing, dipping spirits of the Poudre and finally absorb the peace and song and joy that I know will sustain me through the inevitable winter ahead.

# Following the River
## Veronica Patterson

*Veronica Patterson is the author of two full-length collections of poetry—*How to Make a Terrarium *and* Swan, What Shores?*—as well as a chapbook of prose poems,* This Is the Strange Part. *This poem is rooted in her move to Colorado, where she became familiar with her husband's family that is five generations in the area and long involved with water—ditch companies, farming, irrigation. As she says, this new relationship with water made her want to "know and serve the land where I live."*

> *Freedom is not following a river.*
> *Freedom is following a river*
> *though, if you want to.*
> —William Stafford, "Freedom"

On my first visit to Colorado, I answered the phone and took a message for my future father-in-law. The caller said, "Ask him to call me if he has an extra 12 acre-feet of water." Puzzled, I wrote it down. After I moved here, at a citizen planning meeting, few knew where the river went after it came out of the canyon. One woman who just moved here saying, "We flew in and I said, 'Look at all those lakes. It's like Minnesota.'" Watching snow fall in the mountains, thinking of summer. Ditch companies. Irrigation boots. The idea of making a lake. Regard for a tree. Trying to follow the river through town and out onto the plains. Buildings and roads obscure it. *Where did it go?* Finding a place to climb down to it. Bringing some home in a jar.

**What a Water Fight Used to Be**
Pistols. Clear plastic. If you got a good one, reliable, accurate, you kept it for next summer. Balloons. How full was too full varied by shape and type. You had to gauge rubber quality. The physics of toss, arc, impact.

Where to drop from. On whom. In the plastic pool, the quick flat of the hand for maximum spray and impact. And the fine motor coordination of thumb on hose nozzle, the hard narrow stream, the target dismayed. With a sprinkler, the dash to center, foot suppressing the fountain, luring a dry victim close. Running. When it rained, damming the gutter above your dam. Thoughtless.

# Whitewater Rafting on the Cache la Poudre During a Mountain Storm

Ruth Obee

*Ruth Obee is the author of three collections of poetry and a literary biography of the noted black South African political dissident and writer Es'kia Mphahlele. She has accompanied her husband, a former senior diplomat, to posts in Africa and South Asia where they lived for more than two decades. She then returned to the West with a renewed sense of place and a passion to help preserve it. She was inspired to write this poem by a near-death, whitewater-rafting experience in Nepal; an abiding interest in chaos theory; and, last but not least, a profound desire to help preserve Colorado's last remaining wild river, the Poudre.*

> *Order floats in disorder.*
> —Ilya Prigogine

Lightning charts
its course,
then fills it in with light
like Indian filigree.

Even the single beat
of a monarch's wing
eventually touches El Niño.

The smaller the measure the greater
the complexity in the rough, rain-slanted asymmetries
of the pine-Gothic ridges of the Rocky Mountain peaks.

We know that a trapped proton
can never be seen. Its singularity will remain
un-fingerprinted.

Yet in the midst of nonequilibrium,
a tendency persists to seek out order
on some unexplored shore.

But who can ever graph, test and confirm
the particulate matter of love?
Who can explain the spontaneous combustion of laughter?

Order floats in disorder
like a raft in rapids-churning whitewater
on the Cache la Poudre during a mountain storm.

To be a part of a place, you must reduce it
to its smallest detail …
… know the kind of leaves that fall
from a tree by their sound.

**PART 3**

# Spiral of Our Life

We come and go, but the river remains forever (we hope). In this part, the writers and poets reflect on the Poudre over time. Euro-Americans arrived on the scene here around two hundred years ago. Since that time, the Poudre has changed dramatically. On the scale of one human life, too, change can be seen—not so much from the Poudre itself, but from the viewpoint of the observer. People go to the river during different stages of their life, and they have different river experiences. We seem to use the flowing river as a backdrop, or a gauge, to see how we are growing and learning. Writer-geologist Ellen Wohl describes the physical change of the North Fork of the Poudre after a dam breach, by saying, "I watched the river being reborn." For psychotherapist, Carl Nassar, the change is more internal: "As we run side by side, I let the river in."

# Pass
## Christopher Mulrooney

*Christopher Mulrooney has written poems and translations in*
Eclipse, Crate, The Drunken Boat, Color Wheel, *and* Voices Israel;
*and a volume of verse, notebook, and sheaves. The inspiration for this*
*poem came from abandoned buildings in downtown Los Angeles that*
*reminded him of river canyons.*

roaring Frenchmen knew these waters
between those Alpine meadows
curious and ornate
and straight-flecked
ornamentation of those
crystalline structures
the sort of thing
bounders write about
as curios

# The Lady's Last Dance
## Mark Easter

*Mark Easter is a botanist who lives and writes near the Cache la Poudre River. He lives for wild places, and for the day when life will be restored to the rivers of the Front Range. There was a time when the words "dams," "ditches," and "acre feet" were unknown to the people who lived near the Cache la Poudre River. This story is about the Hayden Geological Survey party of 1869 and one of its members, Henry Wood Elliott, who made detailed etchings of the Poudre during that Survey. Elliot was one of the last people who saw the river as it used to be. Following Mark's essay, Elliott's etchings appear along with photographs taken by Mark and Tim Vaughan of the same scenes 136 years later.*

I t was the stuff dreams were made of. To travel the Colorado frontier and fill oneself up with wild, open country. Every day would bring discovery, adventure, and calculated risk. You would drink straight from the rivers and sleep under overhangs. Prairies overflowing with game would ignite your imagination. Outrageous, vagrant canyons would beckon you deep into the unknown, where the air had never held the stench of roads, and waters had never pooled behind the obscenity of dams.

In 1869, Henry Wood Elliott had the chance to live that dream. During one long, glorious summer and autumn, he worked for Ferdinand V. Hayden on the first official U.S. Survey of Colorado's Front Range, traveling on horseback from Cheyenne down to Santa Fe and then back up the Rio Grande. He made over 400 sketches along the route, including what may be the oldest surviving images of the valley of the Cache la Poudre River, where I live.

There was no published map of their entire route other than smatterings of greasy paper outlining the Overland Trail from Cheyenne to Denver, the mudslide tracks to the gold fields, and the Santa Fe Trail well to the south. Elliott, a Smithsonian Institution artist retained by Hayden as a technical illustrator, became the first person ever to comprehensively document the rivers and mountains of Colorado's Front Range. He was twenty-three years old.

It was the summer of any young man's dreams. Or so I once thought.

————

We now know much of that summer's task and the landscape through which they traveled, but we know little of the hearts of the men who fulfilled it. The survey results are published in an official report to the U.S. Congress, sparingly titled (for its time) *Preliminary Field Report of the United States Geological Survey of Colorado and New Mexico, 1869*, by F. V. Hayden. In it, Hayden laid out in notably optimistic language the economic potential of the Front Range in terms of minerals for development and soils and irrigation water for farming. Its timing could not have been more auspicious. The Civil War had been over for only five years. Colorado was in the midst of its first of many mineral strikes. The land rush frenzy whipped up by the Homestead Act, and the completion of the Union Pacific railroad, was in full flood. Congress was fully committed to developing the West to spur on an economy devastated by the war between the states, and there was a nearly complete vacuum of scientific knowledge about the Western lands the country felt it owned. Hayden, who was renowned for his work surveying the upper Missouri River and the Black Hills, stepped in to fill that void, and Elliot was swept up in the task.

I have pictured many times the survey's journey to my mountain-and-plains valley. After months of preparations and weeks of travel from the East Coast, I see the survey team boarding the freshly painted cars of the Union Pacific in Omaha, and speeding West at the previously unheard-of speed of forty miles per hour. They were a generous mix of experience and naïve optimism. There were field geologists Hayden hired from the University of Pennsylvania, where he taught, and old camp tenders and mavericks, dependable men left over from the beaver trade, whom Hayden had worked with for years on other surveys. Then there was Elliott—the artist cum scientist, self taught in illustration and the only trained biologist on the staff.

I imagine them first seated among the other paying passengers, their hats held in their laps with fingers blackened by too many frostbitten winters. But I picture the crowded car getting the best of them, so they head back to the freight car that held their instruments and gear. They opened the doors wide and spread themselves out on tarps, watching the land rush by as the telegraph line dipped and swayed its way across the Great American Prairie. Coal smoke whipped by the door. They stopped now and then to throw off mail and take on water at side tracks crowded by oxen-pulled freight wagons loaded with bison hides, dried tongue, and most notably, bison bones, awaiting the next eastbound train to take their goods to market. Most of Hayden's men knew the country, and perhaps some of the men disliked the pace of the car and the pace of change that came with it. They recalled that just a few years before, the journey that now took them two days had taken weeks to complete, when vast bison herds still blackened the plains. Towns were now springing up along the route, and they were rarely out of sight of sod homesteads, livestock, or grain fields.

Hearing them talk, did Elliott ache to have come earlier, before the Cheyenne and Lakota wars heated up, to roam the plains with tipi-dwelling nomads? Homesteaders, rapacious disease, market hunting, and the U.S. Cavalry slammed shut the door to any such ambition. The year 1869 on the American Great Plains marked one of the most rapid periods of cultural and ecological change for any place on earth before that day, or since. The Cheyenne and Lakota were locked in the last throes of their struggle for a traditional life, and the game animals were nearly gone.

After arriving in Cheyenne, there would have been guides to meet, wagons and teams and mounts to assess, supplies to sort and load. Then finally, after all the work and planning and anxiety, with his heart in his throat, Elliott was riding south through a country of short grass, prickly pear, and long, gleaming vistas. Three days later, at the end of a long, hot day of survey work, the crew came across the Cache la Poudre, a flooding, bucking, clear-water river galloping out of a canyon of sandstone and granite. They settled into camp on an open bench above the river, a half mile or so from the fledgling town of LaPorte.

Hayden described the valley:

> *This stream, from the point where it issues from the mountains, near Laporte, to its junction with the Platte, a distance of thirty-five miles, runs through a very pretty fertile valley, which averages, perhaps, two miles or more in width, being narrow near the mountains and expanding as it recedes from them. The bottom-land of the valley is flanked on the north side by a rolling, irregular ridge, and on the south side by a somewhat level terrace of moderate elevation. The stream, at Laporte, is about twenty-five yards in width, clear and rapid, affording a sufficient supply of water and ample descent for irrigating the bottoms and ridges or terraces which border it.*

The words "very pretty fertile valley" are practically the only extraneous words not devoted to technical geology in the survey report, and so this is how I picture that evening, camped on a bench above the river. After dinner, with the horses fed and camp-chores settled, Elliott spread out a robe on a patch of buffalo grass, sketch board and pencils in hand. It was too warm in the silky June air to sit near the fire. Hayden and others walked along the river with a group of local homesteaders, discussing irrigation. The cook sang softly to himself nearby while he laid out the morning sourdough. Late that night, the scent of an errant grizzly by the river sent the horses on the picket line into a lather. As Elliott stood calming his mounts under the crystalline sky, a wolf cried from up on the hogback.

———

Elliott was not new to exploration. At age nineteen, he had traveled to the Bering Sea on an expedition to lay a telegraph wire from Alaska to the Kamchatka Peninsula. While sailing north from Seattle he would have seen rivers rivaling the Ohio, a river he certainly knew. But the Ohio was a settled river, no longer wild. The Pacific Northwest, on the other hand, provided wildness in spades. The route was lined with villages of strange people living in colorful longhouses marked by superbly crafted totems. Massive floods poured out of tidewater glaciers, dumping tons of silt each minute. Salmon, halibut, shellfish, and sea mammals were unbelievably abundant. But change was already being felt in the region—many native villages on the route had been wiped out by smallpox and measles. Centuries of exploitation had led to the demise and near extinction of sea otters by the time of his journey. In 1867, two years after Elliott traveled through, Russia sold Alaska to the United States, at least in part because of the recent collapse of the sea otter trade and the loss of native trappers to disease. White and native trappers alike were turning to other sea mammals, fur seals in particular. The fur seal in the Bering Sea would figure prominently in Elliott's future.

It may be impossible to know if he considered these things as he sketched the scenes along and near the Poudre River. The survey report indicates that Hayden and staff geologists visited copper mines up the Poudre Canyon and discussed irrigation and farms with homesteaders during the days. The report offers no sketches above what is now called the Bellevue Dome. Elliott must have stayed in the valley. He would have seen that the wooded bottomlands had been cut, and perhaps heard reports of miners and railroad workers cutting timbers and ties from up the canyon.

One particularly intriguing line in the report stands out. On July 3, the day they left for parts south, Hayden wrote:

> *This valley is one of the most fertile in Colorado. The present year, there has been so much rain that irrigation has been unnecessary. The bottom lands are about two miles wide, and thickly settled from mouth to source. The grass is unusually fine this year everywhere.*

Irrigation was "unnecessary." Other documents describe the dozens of diversions already built to displace water to the farmers' thirsty crops during the driest part of the year. Farmers told Hayden that the rivers regularly ran dry out on the plains during the late summer, and Hayden reports this tidbit as if it were a simple fact of nature, either ignoring or ignorant of the role that irrigation diversions played in such an extraordinary event. Instead, he wrote a long speculation supporting the theory that rain followed the plow on Colorado's Front Range, urging

Congress to appropriate money for a scientific study of the principle. A century and a half later, we now know better.

So what does Elliott's sketch show us today? After a wet spring, the river was near the end of its seasonal uprising from the abundant melting snows of its headwaters. No water was being diverted for irrigation. Elliott may have documented the very last undiverted, unambiguous flood of the Cache la Poudre River. It was the lady's last dance.

———

In 1871, two years to the week from the day Elliott sketched the view of the Poudre River valley from Bingham Hill, he would be entering the spectacular Yellowstone River Valley as official illustrator for the now famous Hayden Survey of what would become the world's very first national park. Several of Elliott's sketches and one watercolor painting remain from that journey, but they were nearly eclipsed by the images of two guest artists—the painter Thomas Moran and the photographer William Henry Jackson. Combined, the work of the three created a public furor over the wonders and beauty of the land. Their artwork alone may have led to the park decree.

At the time of the survey, bison and plains elk were nearing extinction. They survived in refugia and a few remote herds such as those found in Yellowstone. Elliott, an employee of the fledgling Smithsonian Institution, must have known of the bison's decline and the effect it was having on native peoples and the ecosystem of the Great Plains. There were reports already that the passenger pigeons that literally darkened the skies of his childhood, with single flocks numbering in the billions of birds, were now becoming rare. Elliott's was perhaps the first in a long succession of generations for which there was one common, binding experience—the loss of nature. Elliott must have seen it, must have *felt* the urgency of it as he traversed the plains and witnessed the rush of development to lands that just years earlier had been wild. Grasslands littered with bison dung were now littered with bison bones, and even those were being gathered, ground, and sold as fertilizer.

The year after the Yellowstone survey, Elliott made still another remarkable journey. He traveled once again to the Bering Sea, to the

Pribilof Islands—a remote cluster far out into waters described by the naturalist George Steller as "seas of constant storm." Working for the Smithsonian, but as an agent of the Treasury Department, he lived off-and-on for three years among the natives and white Russian trappers and traders to document the natural history and economics of the fur seal. He lived in a sod hut after the local fashion; wore local clothes; lived on seal, halibut, and hardtack like everybody else. His many watercolors and sketches from that time are defining pieces in the historical ethnography of Alaska. In one, we see Pribilof natives harpooning walrus. Others show the fantastically stormy landscape with fur seal rookeries in the foreground.

Perhaps his greatest contribution from that time, though, was a book. *The Seal-Islands of Alaska* is a remarkable piece of writing, with richly drawn sketches of the landscape, people, and wildlife of the islands as well as the requisite economic analysis of the fur trade required by his employer. It set the stage, however, for an even more remarkable act that would be the pinnacle of his career and inspire generations of conservationists. At the time of his visit, Elliott counted at least four million fur seals in the Pribilof Islands alone. When he returned the next decade, they were almost gone.

———

At the urging of colleagues, Elliott returned to the Pribilofs in 1884. Perhaps if we could see into Elliott's heart at the time, we would know that he too felt the shock and deep loss that so many others experience when confronted with the reality of extinction. The fur seal population of the Pribilofs was down to the tens of thousands, possibly hundreds of thousands, and was plummeting under brutal, relentless hunting pressure. Polar bears, numbering in the hundreds on St. Matthew's Island nearby, were completely gone. Elliott did what many people would have done under the circumstances: He conducted his scientific survey with conspicuous attention to detail and accuracy, and then started writing letters and speaking publicly for regulation of fur seal and sea otter hunting. The fact that these animals' populations spanned international borders with Russia complicated matters. Nobody responded. Americans had no predominant conservation ethic at the time. The fur seal population continued its death spiral downward. Then Elliott did something that few people do when faced with the prospect of failure—he kept at it.

Elliott became known for his strident stand on the fur seal trade. He lobbied Congress, spoke to presidents, and infuriated those in the business of trading fur seal hides. He spoke scientific truth to power. Slowly, the tide began to change as the burgeoning rarity of pelts made its presence known in the fur markets. People who had been ignoring Elliott finally began to connect the dots.

Congress finally acted, and Elliott wrote the majority of the fur seal treaty of 1911. It was the first international treaty protecting any species of wildlife. It banned all hunting of fur seals (by then very nearly extinct) and sea otters (widely believed to be extinct already) and empowered Russian and U.S. officials to arrest, fine, and jail or deport anybody caught harming them. The treaty worked, and the promising groundswell of public support for conservation led to the eventual recovery of fur seals and sea otters, which slowly expanded outward from the few, remote refugia in the Aleutian Islands where they clung to existence.

———

History records this act of conservation, but it does not record its heart. Elliott lived another twenty years before dying in his home. We do not know if he learned of the success of his actions before he died. I would like to think that he did. I picture him in his twilight years, taking visits from scientists in the orchard his father established and which he, his wife, and sons still maintained, discussing the latest census figures. I see them strolling, tumblers of bourbon in their hands, amidst a spray of white apple blossoms not unlike the froth of the Pacific Ocean against some Aleutian Island reef. Some young scientist in the group, already an accomplished photographer, snaps a photo of Elliott arguing some fine detail about fur seal biology. And somewhere, on some remote island near the Alaska mainland, a mated pair of sea otters brings a set of new pups into the world, the first there in a century.

––––––––

History also records the decline of our rivers, but it barely records their hearts. By the time of Elliott's second census in the Pribilofs, Colorado had become a state and the residents of LaPorte, Fort Collins, and area farmers were stripping off 100 percent of the Cache la Poudre's flows every year. By the time of the fur trade treaty of 1911, massive trans-basin water diversion projects were in the works. By Elliott's death in 1930, there were dozens of permanent dams and diversions on the Poudre alone. At least two fish species native to Colorado's Eastern Plains had been extirpated, and the greenback cutthroat trout was on a slippery slope downward. In such a short time, the life span of a good man, barely the twitch of a geologic eye, Colorado's rivers were transformed from rich, wild, native things of uncommon beauty and grace, into depleted, stinking ditches.

When I first saw Elliott's sketch of the Arkansas River where it leaves the Rocky Mountains, my own heart stopped beating for a moment. It captures one of the enduring images of the American West, an image approaching mythology—that of wilderness. Wilderness still exists in many places. In 1869 on the Colorado Front Range, it was retreating before a hurricane of change. Our rivers were swept up in the storm.

It seems strange to me now, as I write this, that in such a preindustrial time, when photography was in its infancy as an art form or scientific tool, when the automobile was unknown and radio was some vague engineer's dream, that our rivers—such an enduring element of wildness—were already tumbling toward oblivion. Their headwaters were clear-cut. Their gravel bottoms were upturned for gold as if by some enormous plow. They were stripped of their waters—their life—for irrigation. Superfund sites were already in the making. Elliott saw all of this. In his sketches, he gave us a flurry of landscapes and optimistic pieces early in the survey. Then, as he progressed south, he focused on more technical illustrations and fewer landscapes, perhaps liking less and less of what he saw. He would have witnessed the forests' slopes laid bare by the miner's axe, the putrid water downstream of overflowing gold camps, farmers fertilizing their river-flooded fields with the bones of bison and elk.

So perhaps Elliott's first night on the Cache la Poudre was different from what I originally thought, and different from Elliott's own dreams. On the train ride west, and around the evening campfires, the survey party would have talked about the winds of change blowing upon the land. There were older men among them, veterans of the fur trade. One of them might have wintered along the Poudre during the 1830s with a band of Arapaho. He might have described for them the stately cottonwood groves, the abundance of beaver, elk, bison. He might have told them of the lovely river, its clean gravel bars and velvety waters like a freshet straight from heaven. Elliott might have built an image of his own, and he couldn't wait to see the place.

Then the survey arrived, to find the cottonwoods cleared for firewood and corrals. The valley benches were grazed by cattle and sheep. Rude ditches fanned out from the remains of last year's brush diversion dams, prepared to take water to the grain fields sprouting in the rich bottomland soil. He may have asked his survey partner, the man who wintered here, *Is this the place you lived?* But the man's face had become like a storm cloud over the foothills, and so Elliott left him alone. That night, perhaps Elliott lay in his bedroll, confused and doubting, and worried for his country.

# The Cache la Poudre in 1869 and 2005

Drawings by E. T. Elliott
Photographs by Mark Easter and Tim Vaughan

"Foot Hills of the Rocky Mountains at Cache la Poudre, C.T. (Colorado Territory)," by E. T. Elliott, early July 1869. This was likely the first camp made by Hayden's party when they arrived in the valley. What is striking about this image is what Elliott put in, but also what he left out. Elliott shows some livestock, however he retained only vague hints of buildings and homes. Hayden described the area this way: "This valley is one of the most fertile in Colorado. The present year, there has been so much rain that irrigation has been unnecessary. The bottom lands are about two miles wide, and thickly settled from mouth to source."

2005

"Laporte on Cache la Poudre, Colorado," by E. T. Elliott, early July 1869. The river appears to be just past the spring flood stage. Conservative estimates put flow rate at over 2,500 cubic feet per second, which would have been common during spring floods at the time, but which is rarely, if ever, achieved today.

2005

"Looking into the valley of the Cache la Poudre from behind the Hog Backs," by E. T. Elliott, early July 1869. Elliott likely composed this sketch on site and sketched in rough details, then finished it in a studio in Denver the following winter. Hayden was probably visiting copper mines up the canyon and coal mines near Laporte on the day this sketch was made.

2005

"2 miles South of Laporte, Colorado," by E. T. Elliott, early July 1869. It depicts travelers along the old Glade Road before it was inundated by Horsetooth Reservoir. The notch in the hogback in the distance is now filled by Soldier Canyon Dam.

2005

# Five Haiku for Cache la Poudre River
## Patricia Nolan

*Patricia Nolan has been an educator and white-water river guide. She now paddles in special places to photograph and write essays and poems about the beauty and essentiality of water. She is a member of Poetry West at Colorado College and has nine poems forthcoming in various collections. Her books include* An Interpretive Guide to Farish Recreation Area, Farish Camp Cookbook, *and* Pikes Peak River Runners Cookbook.

### Waves

Spiral of our life
A river flowing freely
Continuity.

### Orgasm

Adrenaline rush
Pulling, bracing down the falls
Rejuvenation.

### Strength

Canyon walls so strong
Embrace new serenity
Healing pain and fear.

**Lessons**

Steven's Gulch quiet
I listen to your message
cheering, joyful, free.

**Future**

We can move toward peace
In the new millennium
Respect, care for earth.

# Pulse of the River
### Ellen Wohl

*Ellen Wohl is a professor of geology at Colorado State University. She has lived in Fort Collins since 1989 and used proximity to the Front Range to study the processes and forms of rivers in the upper South Platte drainage, including the Poudre. Other research has taken her to field sites throughout North America, Central America, Asia, Europe, Africa, and the Middle East. She is the author of* Rain Forest into Desert, Virtual Rivers, *and* Disconnected Rivers. *Her essay, "Pulse of the River," resulted from several years of research in Phantom Canyon along the North Fork Poudre River, where she watched the river recover following the release of a large quantity of sediment from Halligan Reservoir.*

The first stop is always the gate. As I step out of the car, the wind instantly reminds me that I have left town. Most days, a forceful presence knocks me partly off balance—the wind has a long fetch here, blowing across miles of high, gently undulating grasslands. I twirl the combination lock and wrestle with the heavy, awkward catch as I swing the gate open to drive through.

I close the gate and drive down the familiar gravel road. On the western horizon the Medicine Bow Mountains rise white into the blue sky. In spring and early summer, the plateau beneath them lies vibrant green. Red-winged blackbirds call from creases that hold small wetlands. Among the grasses, clusters of white sand lily blossoms hug the ground. Wallflowers raise spikes of bright yellow, and the slender green stems of western spiderwort carry delicate, deep-blue flowers.

I pull up at the visitor center of The Nature Conservancy's Phantom Canyon Preserve, located about thirty miles north of Fort Collins. As a fluvial geomorphologist, I study the physical processes of rivers, and the North Fork Poudre River where it flows through Phantom Canyon is a favorite field site. I have been coming here since 1996, a privileged visitor. I came initially because of an unfortunate choice, but I keep coming for more subtle and complex reasons.

The unfortunate choice was not mine. In late September 1996 the North Fork Poudre Irrigation Company, which operates Halligan Dam just upstream from the preserve, released an estimated 250,000 cubic feet of sediment into the North Fork Poudre River, and then shut off the flow.

Halligan is a "fill and spill" dam. The irrigation company can release some water through outlet valves at the base of the dam. If this level of release is not fast enough to prevent the reservoir from rising during spring snowmelt flows, the waters eventually overtop the dam and spill downstream. Less than five miles downstream from the dam, the irrigation company has a canal that can siphon off some water. This water is sent in surface canals and tunnels that burrow beneath hills to the next reservoir downstream, where it supplies irrigated agriculture on the plains. The usual practice is to drain Halligan Reservoir in late fall, shut off almost all flow during the winter, and then let the reservoir fill during spring and store water for release late in the summer growing season. Until The Nature Conservancy purchased a tiny minimum flow during the winter, the irrigation company shut off the flow completely from about late September to February or March, which caused the North Fork downstream from Halligan to dry up into a series of deep, still pools in which the fish holed up for the winter.

Halligan Reservoir was gradually filling with sediment. Concerned with loss of storage capacity, the irrigation company decided to release a slug of sediment that had accumulated against the dam. This was fine sediment—the gravel-to-clay sized particles that could travel all the way through the long, winding reservoir to the dam. Releasing this sediment into a steep, swiftly flowing river like the North Fork would not necessarily cause a problem, as long as there was sufficient flow to keep the sediment moving downstream and dispersed along many miles. But in September 1996 the water stopped. The sediment stopped, too, piling up along nearly seven miles of the river.

Immediately downstream from the dam, pools that had been eleven feet deep filled to the brim with sediment. The steeply undulating streambed of shallow riffles alternating downstream with deep pools became a planar bed of mud. Progressively less sediment filled the pools downstream to about three miles below the dam, where real, watery pools still existed after the sediment release.

To its surprise, the irrigation company had a public relations mess on its hands. The Colorado Division of Wildlife did a body count of the dead fish that they could find at the surface—4,000—and local newspapers picked up the story. Anglers and environmentalists expressed anger. The irrigation company retained a lawyer and claimed that the dead fish had come over the 110-foot-high dam or through the outlet valves: "Those were our fish to kill."

I visited the canyon with fishery biologists from the university and the Division of Wildlife. I had never been to the canyon—never heard of it—but the biologists wanted some estimate of how long it would take the river to move all the excess sediment downstream. I walked along the channel in hip waders. Slimy clay and silt draped everything below the high-water mark. Where pools had been, the deep accumulations of mud were liquid and shaky as quicksand. The unseasonably hot air stank of rotting fish, and the scavengers were feasting. Footprints of black bear and mountain lion zigzagged across the firmer mud along the stream banks. Turkey vultures and hawks tracked my progress. A Nature Conservancy employee who accompanied us pointed out the cliffside nest of a pair of golden eagles.

It seemed to be an environmental tragedy. All of the fish were introduced species, but they had been a self-sustaining population here far from the stocking trucks of fish hatcheries. The Nature Conservancy worried about the many pairs of ouzels that nest along the canyon, feeding on the abundance of aquatic insects that live in the clear, cold waters of the North Fork. Everyone asked me, How long? When will the river be healthy again? I had little idea. I thought maybe ten years, depending on the flows next spring and summer. Meanwhile, I marveled at everything.

Phantom Canyon is one of those secret places, so hidden that you might literally be on the canyon rim before realizing that a canyon existed. The walls drop down from the plateau nearly vertically, and until you are on the rim you hear no roar of water from below. This place— and I was so indignant that I had never heard of this wonderland so close to my home in Fort Collins—was startlingly beautiful. The orange and pink granite of the canyon walls rises steeply toward the blue sky. A few tall ponderosa pines grow along the river and in shadowed moist portions of the walls, but mostly the terrain is open. Tough shrubby mountain mahogany and small clusters of juniper and pinyon pine rise above the grasses, which were bleached golden that September day.

The rest of that autumn and early winter, I enlisted a succession of graduate students to help with the field work. We surveyed the first few miles of the channel, crawling unsteadily on boards across the quaking mudflats as we probed down to the original cobble and boulder bed with long pieces of rebar. We collected bags of sediment to analyze back in the lab, dug into the riffle gravels until we reached a level where the reservoir sediment had not penetrated, and set up sampling cross sections for measuring water and sediment flows next spring. I never lacked for volunteers.

I began to take possession of the canyon in my imagination. I named our sampling sites the Goose Pool (Canada geese nested there, pugnacious birds that hissed if I got too close), the Ouzel Pool (guess what nested there?), the Tick Pool (this was the first stream crossing at the base of the trail, where the ticks took advantage of us as we sat on a grassy bank to put on waders), and the Fish Pool (the first pool at which we found living fish in our progress down the river). I noticed more details. Each time I descended the canyon I crossed a dramatic line between the arid valley walls where cacti grew among pieces of desiccated rotting wood and papery lichens covered the rock outcrops, and the softer, more-lush vegetation and deeper shades of green along the river corridor. I took time to see the gently curving parallel striations that the processes of weathering had etched into the canyon walls, and the graffiti of white, green, gray, and orange lichens growing over them. I found a dead owl and marveled at the bird's massive talons and enormous eye sockets.

The mud hardened and cracked. Snow began to fall and ice formed thin milky white plates that crackled beneath us as we walked along the channel margins. One cold day just before Thanksgiving I walked across the surface of a frozen pool, watching in fascination as the ice undulated in front of me, until the ice broke and a student fished me out. With the deepening cold and darkness of winter, snow and ice sealed the channel and sediment movement ceased. I left the quiet river for the winter.

The river began to flow again while spring was still only a hopeful dream. The irrigation company partially opened the outlet valves starting in February, and in March they gave us an experimental flow, quickly raising and then lowering the flow levels so that we could measure how sediment transport and storage changed. We all—the river, the scientists, the irrigation company—got very lucky, for 1997 was a good flow year. Plenty of snowmelt swelled Halligan Reservoir and the irrigation company brought the flows up.

As water began to flow among the half-buried boulders of the streambed, the finest sediment washed off in a flush of turbid brown water. The submerged boulders began to give up their little hoards of sediment—pockets of sand and gravel that had been stored in the lee created by each large boulder—as the water continued to rise. The water kept rising and overtopped the dam, the flow stepping up every few days and swirling another pulse of fine sediment before it. The steadily churning water, released from the dam without sediment, began to empty the upstream pools of their accumulated sediment, too. Slowly a domino-like wave of pool-emptying water moved downstream until most of the original pool volume was restored.

Coming every other day to sample the swiftly rising flow felt like being introduced to a new river each time. I started with a dry, rocky streambed, easy to walk across. Then a shallow flow inscrutable as milky black tea, only a few protruding boulders to help guide me as I stumbled across the uneven surface. Then a deep, swift flow the color of cola, so that I had to shuffle around to find a stable boulder and then brace a foot against it before taking the next step. Soon the water lapped up the banks, submerging the base of the river birch and alder at the channel's edge, and flowed so fast that I fixed my sight on a point ahead and leaned into the flow, moving in careful counterpoints of balance. At the peak, I could only venture to the edge of the swiftest flow, the cold water buffeting my body and gripping me so firmly in my neoprene chest waders that I felt heavy and sluggish as I re-emerged on the bank.

As the flow came up and the sediment left, the creatures of the river returned. I envied the ouzels their strength and agility as I watched them plunge into the same churning water through which I slipped and lurched. The ouzels had good feeding, for the aquatic insects were recolonizing the damaged river by their own mysterious pathways. The invertebrates did not return in their pre-1996 abundance and diversity for a few years, but they did return. Canada geese nested along the river, as did mergansers. And as the flows declined again at the end of the summer, I surprised trout struggling through shallow riffles.

I watched the river being reborn.

That first summer of field work provided a lot of data, and answered some questions about how much sediment the river could carry. But so many questions remained. What controls where the pools form? How fast is the river cutting down into the bedrock of the canyon floor? How does water move through the complex topography of pools and riffles and past big boulders? How has the dam changed the pulse of the river? What sizes of flow should The Nature Conservancy ask for in order to restore the river?

The answers to these questions are multifaceted, but they are not exactly the subtle and complex reasons for my repeated visits to the canyon. Some of the reasons are quite straightforward. The preserve has limited access, and I feel comfortable leaving survey benchmarks or equipment down in the canyon for years at a time (only once did someone—apparently a black bear—rip open one of the storage boxes and toothfully sample some of the contents). Although dammed, the North Fork has few of the other human effects that make it so complicated to study river processes along the other rivers of the Colorado Front Range. If I find few pools along Clear Creek west of Golden, for example, is that because of nineteenth-century beaver trapping, contemporary flow regulation, historical placer and dredge-boat mining, roads and railroads along the river, urbanization in the drainage, or something else? The variables in Phantom Canyon, on the other hand, are few. Phantom Canyon is also close—only about a 45-minute drive from home—and the hike in is steep, but short. The Nature Conservancy welcomes the enhanced understanding of river processes that results from my work. Ultimately, I think I keep coming back to Phantom Canyon because it feels like my secret place.

Every child seems to have a secret place, whether it's outdoors, in the home, or simply a place that they go to in their mind. Many of us lose that feeling as adults, but I doubt that we lose the ability to feel delight when we stumble onto a secret place.

Phantom Canyon is a well-used preserve. A student intern lives in a house on the canyon rim each summer, and volunteers lead guided natural history hikes along the trails through the preserve. Volunteers fight invasive weeds, conduct bird counts, or help the conservancy in other ways on most weekends. Fishermen vie in a raffle for a chance to fish a half-mile length of the river. But I never feel the pressure of people when I visit the canyon. I avoid weekends, and once I drop below the canyon rim, I rarely see another human. What I do see, season after season and year after year, is the pulse of the river.

I see the seasonal changes. Furry pale-blue pasqueflowers give way to the showy greenish-yellow blooms that nearly hide the tiny pincushion cacti. Yellow warblers mark the start of summer, flitting among the bee-buzzing masses of white flowers in the chokecherry stands along the river. In the cold shadows of springtime, I climb carelessly down steep bedrock slopes knobbled by pink crystals of feldspar and milky white quartz. Under summer's heat, I move watchfully across the same slopes, always alert for the breath-stopping buzz of a rattlesnake. Exotic cheatgrass changes from pliant, soft green stalks in early summer to sharp seeds that bristle into my socks in autumn. The river rises, feeding ouzels and mergansers, then falls again, and the protruding boulders look like ribs on a thin animal. The slender spring-time deer with ragged coats look plump and well-furred by the time the rabbitbrush forms yellow sunbursts above the dried grasses. Snow flurries replace the cooling winds of a summer thunderstorm racing down the canyon.

I see the longer, slower changes superimposed on the rhythm of the seasons. In the absence of scouring floods during the drought years after 1997, masses of filamentous algae clog the streambed, like submarine heads of long green hair swaying in the warm, shallow water. The river birch and alder continue to age, slowly dying back, and no new floods come to root them up and deposit sediment and seedlings that will renew the riparian forest. The conservancy burns a patch of river bottom infested with exotic mullein and sprays a patch of exotic thistles with molasses to make them more palatable to a few cows brought down to graze.

This is not a world apart. The river, to some extent, rises and falls to the rhythms set by the men who operate the dam upstream. The plants that can thrive here are those that have withstood grazing in the past, flow regulation at present, perhaps ongoing climate change. Those that come here are largely invasive weeds, at least indirectly assisted by humans. The animals that remain are those that have not been locally hunted to extinction, as was the grizzly bear, the bison, and the wolf.

The idea that Phantom Canyon is wilderness is purely illusion, and yet this is an illusion that I find very difficult to overcome. I am a passive observer in this secret place. I am not responsible for watering the plants or feeding the animals. Humanity *en masse* influences much of what happens here, but I do not control any single entity in this ecosystem. I come, and I forget what paces my life beyond the canyon. I watch a world beyond myself change at its own pace, and I remember how I am enmeshed in and supported by this greater world.

The paradox of Phantom Canyon is the paradox of the world environment; how can each person realize that the immense natural world—which seems to supersede us with its tremendous forces of blizzard and tsunami, tornado and locust migration—is so thoroughly altered by human actions that the decisions we now make as communities and societies determine the future of the natural world in ways that we cannot fully understand?

The pulse of the North Fork Poudre River reflects the things we can directly control—the amount of water released through the dam's outlet valves, the exotic trout introduced to the Colorado Front Range, the sediment trapped behind the dams along the river, the nitrates emitted into the atmosphere from our tailpipes and deposited over the North Fork watershed.

The river's pulse also reflects the things that we do not directly control, but probably indirectly influence—the snowpack that accumulated this year in the headwaters, the stoneflies and caddisflies that migrated into Phantom Canyon, and the seeds dropped from the aging river birch growing along the stream banks. The river has a complicated pulse, with specific events such as the 1996 sediment release or the 1998–2004 drought superimposing an irregular rhythm on the steady beat of the seasons. Like the muscle of a healthy heart, the North Fork can recover from these irregular rhythms. But the more we alter the blood of this heart—the flow of water, nutrients, and sediment along the river—the more we compromise its ability to recover from the irregularities that will always be present.

The 1996 sediment release from Halligan Dam was not the environmental tragedy that it seemed to be at first. Thanks to a good flow year in 1997, most of the sediment was flushed downstream and gradually deposited in smaller accumulations that did not locally wipe out aquatic habitat. The insects, the fish, and the birds eventually came back, although it took years to regain the levels of abundance and diversity present before the sediment release. The sediment release garnered a lot of publicity because it was a catastrophic event—a very quick and obvious change in the river. What is probably more threatening to the river ecosystem, and the pulse of the river, are the gradual, long-term changes that result from flow regulation and water withdrawal. Scientists are just beginning to document these changes.

A riparian ecologist demonstrated the existence of a "seed shadow" downstream from Halligan Dam, where the seeds of riparian trees that normally float downstream to new germination sites are absent because they are trapped behind the dam. The aging riverside forests in the canyon downstream are not being replaced by natural regeneration, and these forests drop leaves and twigs, and whole logs, that form a critical source of nutrients and habitat for insects and fish living in the river. The forests also support beaver, which in turn build small dams and create areas of ponded water that increase the diversity and stability of the river.

Other researchers are measuring the differences in aquatic insect communities on regulated and unregulated rivers in the Colorado Rockies. Fish and ouzels feed on the insects, but we do not yet understand how changes in the species composition of insect communities might influence these predators. A graduate student demonstrated that unregulated rivers in the Front Range tend to contain more wood, which in turn affects the size and spacing of pools. We do not yet understand all the effects of a dam. But we know that interrupting the natural rhythms of water, sediment, nutrients, and seeds moving down the river corridor clearly creates complex effects that only become detectable over a period of decades.

As I sit near the canyon rim, a small hawk unexpectedly soars over a rise next to me, gracefully tilting its body as it traces the contours of the land. The rhythm of its movement is pure beauty, as is the rhythm of the river beneath. I do not want the pulse to stop.

# Poudre River Poem

Ted Lardner

*Ted Lardner teaches writing in Ohio. He lived in Fort Collins from 1977 to 1983. He looked at, rafted once, hitchhiked twice, cried into, and forgot the Poudre River. In his "Poudre River Poem," he remembers one particularly memorable evening alongside it.*

I have to ask all these dead people first, do they mind me skipping by them on the Trailways to Fort Collins, in their rain ditches and mental hospitals, do they mind I talk sweetly about a golden greenish stinky sometimes mountain river with foaming complicated drowning holes and slick fast water through the narrows the campground abductions and blankets under stars with my girlfriend first wife-to-be's hips staggering down on me like an under-pulling what they call them, rafters, back-rolling, how it does it, backs you up under the over-wash, and there were stars out there, I could see them, but they didn't look like any sense could be found in sorting—triangles here, rectangles there. We coiled next to each other and the fire went out and in the quiet the river at the rocks whooshed and purled and didn't care about anything but slanting off the shruggy boulder jam and spreading quiet in the flatlands farther down, out the prairie. There was dust on everything.

# The Mirror in the River

Diane Fromme

*Diane Fromme is a writer and journalist who also enjoys coordinating international exchange students. Her hobbies include cycling, hiking, and volleyball. She is married and resides in Fort Collins. Her family includes her husband, three children (19, 18, and 6), two dogs and two cats. In this essay, she explores how the river has been a catalyst for her own life transformations, providing escape, respite, and strength in the midst of family challenges.*

In the middle of nowhere, completely unannounced, surges the pound and froth of a waterfall, just upriver from an unpretentious building called the Mishawaka Inn. Constructed in 1919 as a family gathering place for food, music, and dance, the Mishawaka continues its musical tradition of almost nine decades by hosting annual summer concerts that feature an eclectic mix of musicians.

The Mish is a natural-pine shanty that houses the only bar and grill within twenty miles on either side. Often stumbled upon by sightseers in the Poudre Canyon, its clientele on any given day can range from ravenous families to beer-drenched bikers to musicians signing autographs on cocktail napkins. On this day, my husband, Brian, and I are heading up the canyon highway with two tickets to hear Chuck Mangione play his big, brassy-horn style of jazz fusion.

Tucked away from the highway's view is the inn's jewel: an oval splat of fresh, green lawn that serves as its amphitheater. A covered wooden bandstand bolstered by sturdy evergreen poles backs to Highway 14's roadside companion, the Poudre River, which flows and gurgles by while intermittent concert blares and wails rise above its presence.

A truly perfect day is ethereal, especially for someone like me whose life is consumed by a high-pressure PR job and the shock of being a new stepmother. But on this day I get a break—the day is filled with air hockey with my quick husband, the bright sun, lemony beer, and the exquisite horns of the Chuck Mangione Band.

For this short while, the Mish lawn is the only place in the world—a respite from the demands of a nontraditional family. I am so tired of doing and giving; here, only the musicians are playing this role. Chuck's eyes are closed as he blows his saxophone from a deep, soulful place, and the other musicians are smiling. Their making of music looks effortless—an illusion for the beholder, like the seeming perfection of certain families. I often idolize this illusion. Many days, the dysfunction in my new family plagues me. But today, the ease and beauty of the music allows me to simply listen, dream, dance, or just be. Fellow audience members are lounging in the sun, or sitting and beating out notes with their fingers. A few people are playing air sax, or celebrating with their entire bodies. We're sharing Alice in Wonderland's fantastical golden afternoon as the lovely, brassy notes hang in the air, then disperse out to the river. I am part of a giant family that is being loved, accepted, entertained.

Since I rarely make time to sit still, I enter the realm of the surreal when I tip my head back in the lawn chair and listen to the master play "Clouds" while watching the clouds float by across the heavens. The keyboards and horns crescendo through an ascending progression of three chords, the third being a musical climax that lifts my dizzy spirit straight to the sky. The lingering chord sends the crowd into a round of whoops and applause. I am laughing and clapping, hanging on to this moment like a child clutching the string of a treasured balloon so that it doesn't become a forgettable dot against the big blue.

Chuck provides humor too. I love the way he refers to his wife, taking a little poke at the complexities of marriage: "She's my *third* wife. She's my *best* wife. And she's my *last* wife," he announces. This brings appreciative laughter and deep-voiced shouts of "YEAH!" from our clan, who easily range in age from twenties to sixties. I feel more secure in this makeshift family than I do in my own, as Chuck exposes his own vulnerabilities and others identify so vocally. We are not alone in our ecstatic joy or our personal pain.

Brian and I look at each other knowingly; we are both on our second marriages.

"Will you be my last wife?" he asks.

"I want to," I reply, with the best knowledge I can summon at the moment.

The extra twist in our marriage is bittersweet—Brian has two lovely young children whose mother died of cancer. None of our foursome has grown comfortable with the new arrangement, and I yearn to deepen my security and pull us all together, though I don't know how.

I cap off the concert with a final coup: In the bar, with the wooden doors open to the deck and the river beyond, I beat Brian at air hockey. Never mind that his reflexes are now dulled by good beer. It's important to me to defeat him in this playful power struggle. At home, I channel energy toward the task of trying to fit in my new family—at being a mom without replacing Mom. Here, I hold raw, fierce focus on something I can call my own—something as simple as the satisfying *pock* of plastic blocking plastic.

Once victory is mine, I indulge in a half-pound, sloppy cheeseburger oozing with ketchup, spicy mustard, mayonnaise, and pickles. Then, we relax on the deck, draping ourselves over white, plastic chairs and sunning in the changing afternoon light. Elongated yellow rafts drift by below. In them, riders in bright blue spray jackets wave from their perches on the rafts' spongy benches. They look happy. I, too, feel a sunburned, spent yet content sensation from a day full of flowing experience instead of rigid schedules and unspoken expectations. Dancing around us in tribute are the spirits of generations who came to the Mishawaka for musical release.

I look over the deck and watch the river. With my roots as a city girl, I understand next to nothing about the dynamics of river flow and current. Yet I can see that in less than half a mile, the river has morphed from a hard glassy waterfall into a smooth fast-running stream. I want to be closer to the river, to feel and hear the water's rush. Without a word of explanation, I seek out some stone-cut earthen stairs down to the gravelly river's edge. I close my eyes and draw in the stinging dampness of fish, moss, and froth. Expansive, deep breathing makes me feel woozy with connectedness. I feel God, the giddiness of music, and the rawness of the river flowing through me in this moment at the Mishawaka Inn. I allow this moment to be the only one that matters.

———

Almost a decade later, I am sitting on my back porch studying a river-rafting brochure. From a recent hike along the Big South trail, I know that the Poudre can transform itself from calm deep pools to urgent whitewater around the next curve. Though armed with this knowledge of the Poudre's schizophrenia, I still have the urge to ride it. With the passing of time, I've become less concerned with doing the responsible things for the family and more interested in creating a little fun.

As a child, I'd had one experience rafting the Columbia that whetted my appetite for more, before fears could creep in to dampen my spirit. Since Brian's children, Brianna and Bud, are now teenagers, I become excited to expose more of my spirit to them through a family trip on the river.

In the early years, they were too young and distrustful to see who I might be. We spent the middle years walking a tenuous tightrope of companionship, with more good times than bad. It was a pleasant though deceiving plateau. We weren't truly close, and yet we often operated like a family unit. Now, approaching the thick of adolescence, Brianna and Bud are on the brink of pulling away again. The time we spend in the raft will be longer than any family dinner we've shared in the last year.

Brianna and Bud are as different as the Hudson River and the Poudre—the older one steady and more thoughtful, and the younger one volatile and more determined. They often make a show of not getting along. I see an opportunity in this event to create some of the family teamwork and harmony that we can't manage to pull off at home. I don't know what's going to happen—how the dynamics might change or affect our patterns and habits—but I'm ready to take the risk. Brian and I choose a half-day Mish Falls trip for this family boat, a run that faces some real Poudre challenges in the form of class III and IV rapids.

On the bus trip upriver, I play a little game where I choose which rafting guide should be in our boat. I pick the stocky guy with the wild

Shirley Temple curls. He's cracking jokes with the novice rafters, wanting to see how far he can push them into believing that the river sucks new blood. I'm looking at 250 pounds of piss and vinegar encased in a sun-ruddy barrel of a body. Burly with confidence, he simultaneously talks, chews gum, and arranges his rafting gear. When we exit the bus and assemble in groups, he saunters over to our family and pumps a meaty hand in greeting. "You're lucky to have me," he says. "Call me Critter."

Meanwhile, I'm quietly reviewing the instructions from the trip talk, reminding myself to wedge my feet into the creases of the raft. On the other hand Bud, fifteen years old, is the kind of person who reinterprets instructions. The first day he ever took Advil, I showed him the dosage on the bottle: "Do not take more than eight in twenty-four hours." He took six, twice. In junior high school, we coached him not to take an inflatable doll to the formal, but later I found his junior high yearbook with the words inked on the inside front cover: "Bud. The doll, dude. That was awesome."

I'm toying with the idea of a quick chalk talk with Bud when Critter floats the raft and we load in. When Critter points Bud to the back of the boat, next to him, I let go of the need to pass on what I think is important. I imagine they'll be fine together. With their defensive-end builds, they look like guardian sumo wrestlers, decked out in three times their normal amount of clothing. Brian and I claim the front bench and Brianna nestles into the middle with a friend. For several minutes, we float peacefully, our two heroic icons providing ballast against the river. Then, with no further warning, we head into the waves. Paddling "forward two" into Zig Zag, the first rapid on this trip, we hear a *thunk* sound. I crane my neck around to see what I believe, yet cannot believe, has happened. Bud is in the water, on the right side of the boat. He's able to keep his paddle and Critter shoots out a stout arm to grab it.

"Hoist yourself right over the side," barks Critter.

"Bud's in the water," I yell to Brian.

"I don't know what to do," he yells back.

"There goes my brother," Brianna says to her friend.

"Back two," shouts Critter. The rest of us push some water forward. Bud grabs the thick, sodden rope that is hanging from the top of the raft. He lets go of the paddle and Critter drops it into the boat. Bud grunts and emits a creaky, bass moan of effort. The current is pushing him back and he's having trouble pulling himself up. His trunk is suspended on the yellow rubber, like a whale splayed out for butchering, while his legs dangle in the water behind him.

If Bud had been at the Mish ten years ago, and had fallen into the river, I would have been more worried about Brian than Bud, watching as he grappled with a precarious situation involving his son. Over the years I've come to care for these kids, and seeing Bud so vulnerable and helpless douses me with waves of fear and compassion. I want to help, but Bud and I don't have that kind of bond where he can look into my eyes and feel reassured. So instead, I too feel helpless and detached, like I do when watching high drama unfold on TV.

Brian and I turn halfway around, our paddles still poised for instructions. Critter clamps one iron hand around Bud's upper arm, and this support seems to give Bud the necessary boost to roll himself into the boat.

I always show concern when Bud is hurt or sick, but I feel that deep down he doesn't register. There is a stoic wall inside him that few, if any, can penetrate with their goodness. A caring gesture ricochets off that wall like a racquetball, and it's hard to predict where it will land. Brian and I check in to hear that Bud's all right, and his response is strictly perfunctory.

Bud has a few minutes to recuperate before our raft plunges into Tunnel Falls, the first of two class IV rapids close together. Abruptly, Critter yells, "Whoa!" Brian and I turn and catch a glimpse of an empty seat on the back of the raft. We've lost Bud again! This time he goes out of sight under the curl of the rapid, finally emerging behind the raft. I look at Brian, eyes wide, searching for answers. Brianna is frowning and doesn't turn around at all. Despite the severity of the situation, a list of habitual reactions runs through my head. "Is he that uncoordinated? Is this some weird way to attract attention? Can't he be serious about anything? What is his problem?" Bud's actions are usually an irresolvable juxtaposition of the predictable and unpredictable.

We experience a pause that seems like minutes, but we can only afford seconds.

Ding Dong is coming up quickly. Through the high river splash, I see Critter lean out the rear of the raft and literally dead-lift Bud back into the boat.

"Here we go!" Critter croaks, without missing a beat. "We need ya dude! Everyone, forward three and back one!"

I know that if Bud had simply floated behind the raft, he wouldn't have caught up with us. He had to be rescued, and no combination of our family members really had the strength or the knowledge to do it. I can't help but wonder how he would have reacted to our attempts— if, even in danger, the wall would have risen too high for us to scale. Thankfully, we have the gift of someone whose help he can accept. I am relieved by Critter's lack of panic, and I marvel at the opportune pairing of this swaggering guide with our family boat. You might call it coincidence, or you might have faith in holy intervention. I truly believe that, though all the river guides are well trained, we are blessed with the *bomb* of the day's crew.

A minute of delay can impact the entire raft's success, and we need as much strength and family unity as possible coming out of Ding Dong. Some rafting companies call this rapid Flip Rock. If you can't turn your boat to the right coming out of Flip Rock, it's very easy to high-side against a sheer wall on the left and flip the entire raft.

Although we know Bud's back in the boat, he seems to be miles away. We are disconnected from his possible pain and his motives, as we prepare for the team task ahead. We are coming together to save our raft from flipping.

After executing a barrage of orders from Critter, the boat merely grazes the granite, emerging from the rapid secure and level. At a calm spot between rapids, we perform a river high-five, whacking all our paddles together above the center of the boat. Stoic despite the drama, Bud says, "I'm fine," and gives us his best for the rest of the ride. Consistent with our family habit of letting charged situations evaporate, no one ever asks him why he fell out of the raft. Later, we find out he was badly bruised, and held his leg stiff for twelve days before feeling better.

Exactly two years and five days after that trip, Bud moves prematurely out of our house. He tells us he wants the chance to do everything on his own. He tells his friends something more: that he can't live with the women in his house. I know he's directing his rebellion at me, because I'm not the woman he wishes were still alive. My hurt snakes down deep and angry. After having given so much, I now have to find a way to let him go, and to admit to the world that I couldn't pull everyone together.

———

There is no family involved in my next rafting journey. June 2004 while the river is running at four-plus feet, I embark on the most exciting Mish Falls trip of all.

On this trip, I am simply Diane. Not wife, not mother, not stepmother, but river goddess and seeker of adventure. Like the magical concert day at the Mishawaka Inn, I am ready to experience whatever the river has in store for me. However, this day carries a distinct separation from the day at the inn. Then, I was running away. Now, I am chasing the healthy, liberating fix I have come to depend on from this river.

My rafting mates are highly motivated too, this being their first rafting experience on any river. I don't have the same history with these guys that I do with my family, and I like it that way. Chris, a volleyball friend, and Kal, our exchange student from Bulgaria, are going to do this trip come cold, rain, lightning, or Armageddon. Good thing. As the bus pulls out of Fort Collins in a misting rain, the thermometer logs 60 degrees, while the river temperature is closer to 35. We are grateful for wetsuits, booties, and spray jackets, soggy as they are from the morning run.

I play the guide game again, and choose Dan from New York City. In the strong, secure spirit of the day, I am sure I won't be denied this geographical connection with my past. Dan sports black, curly hair—a dark contrast to his bright smile. The staff seems excited, rather than nervous, about the height of the river.

When the river runs above four feet, you don't have to worry about dragging your bottom on rocks. Just the opposite, this ride feels like jet skiing waves in the ocean. Avid rafters have described this run at this height as one continuous class IV rapid. Sure enough, we hit nearly constant whitewater through Three Way and Ginsu Corner. We plunge and bounce like rodeo riders, literally tasting the tinny river as it attacks over all sides of the raft. Swallowing the splash and blinded by its height, I am inside the river, and the river is me. We bend with the boat and meld flesh with paddle. At the height of each rapid we are frozen in time, a rendering of absolute unity. On the drops, we whoop from the heady rush of stomach-dropping vertigo. I am strong and independent, like a wild bull, bucking through surges of my true power. Today I am only responsible for myself, and I love this part of me.

The river finally spins out into a calm stretch. We smell burgers and spicy fries cooking as we float by the Mishawaka, waving at the drinkers and party-goers on the weathered deck. Dan and I reminisce about the salty taste of juicy all-beef hot dogs and steaming hot pretzels from New York City street vendors.

I look back at the Mish, imagining those lovely, brassy horn sounds captured in nostalgic bubbles that pop over the river. How uncertain I was then, chasing the illusion of a secure family. How strong I feel now, despite the blinding truth that the illusion is ephemeral. The Mish disappears from view, and the river flows on.

 # Under the Benevolent Influence of a Water Deity

Carl R. Nassar

*Carl R. Nassar traded his tenured faculty position in telecommunications at Colorado State University for new graduate degrees in counseling psychology. He currently works as a psychotherapist at his practice, Heart-Centered Counseling, in Fort Collins. One of his passions is eco-psychology, the healing of individuals by a reclaiming of healthy relationship with the human and the more-than-human world.*

It was a chance encounter on Boulder's Pearl Street when I met a book. I'd had a long silence between impassioned reads. I knew immediately the silence was shattered. *Black Elk Speaks* was this sort of a book.

Literary intimacy ensued: I would gently turn pages; he would share his words with me, touching me deeply. When I listened as *Black Elk Speaks*, I did not hear one story. I heard many. At first blush, I read a narrative speaking to the devastation of a deeply spiritual nation. I listened to the annihilation of a passion and reverence for the web of life that remains the modern world's lost ingredient. I experienced the desolation of a people made for the earth by a people who mistakenly believed the earth was made for them. I cried for a tragedy of planetary proportions.

———

My love for the Poudre began in my belly, before I knew Black Elk spoke.

The abundance of my belly spanned generations. He is my father, I am his son. Excess weight floods our middles, finds comfort there, and leaves thinness elsewhere. My belly is also shaped by career choice.

I am a psychotherapist. Stillness, both of spirit and body, creates a space suited to healing. In short, I move only a little during the day.

Recently, my belly's restoration can be attributed to the Poudre. That, however, is how I met the river, not how I fell in love with it.

————

With *Black Elk Speaks*, my tears were not only for the death of the free American Indian. I was awakening to what I had lost, for what was killed in the American Indian had long been dead in me. I grew up a sickly child, plagued by the two illnesses of our modern civilization: isolation and loneliness. Don't misunderstand. There were plenty of people nearby in my childhood years. Physically together, we were emotional islands.

I did what I could: I hid. I found comfort in books, both of the comic and school variety. In Spider-Man, if only for the twenty minutes a comic book lasted, I confronted my enemies (superhuman), faced my fears (thank God for Spider-Sense), overcame unbelievable odds (every issue), and was crowned hero. In academic books, I found parental praise.

Quickly, I traded in the lonely world of people for the soothing world of books. There, I hid myself from my pain. Secretly, I held out hope that someone would find me, uncover me, and bring me back to a life of communion and community. No one ever did. For years, I lay hidden behind a book.

The slaughter at Wounded Knee, ending *Black Elk Speaks*, represented both reality and personal metaphor: that I had, out of childhood necessity, slaughtered within myself my interconnections with another and all of life, and severed ties with what it means to be a true human being. Black Elk helped reawaken my yearning to be found. I had lost contact with the people and the planet around me. I wanted it all back. Badly.

I cried. I wanted to bring back the free American Indian. I wanted to bring back my indigenous soul, that part longing for the interconnection that makes earth a heaven, without which I live as less than I could.

————

It would be a while before I was healthy enough to meet the river.

To reshape my belly, I began in earnest, running around blocks of Old Town Fort Collins. Three blocks up Park Street, one block over, then three blocks down West. The whole exhausting experience took ten minutes. (In my defense, I feel compelled to explain that these are long blocks, but in truth I don't know that they are.)

Both my female neighbors, to my left and to my right, run, and I hoped they would not notice my premature return filled with panting and out-of-breath gasps. To make appearances worse, because I rarely made sufficient time for the running, I typically ran in what I slept in, PJ bottoms and then a jacket thrown over a PJ top. I owned running shoes I'd bought three years earlier with grand intentions. "These are the kind they wear when they run the Boston Marathon," the salesman reassured me. Seven blocks later, panting in PJs and Adidas, I was far removed from the Wheaties poster boy of the Boston Marathon mold.

———

Through Black Elk, I'd unblocked my longings for connectedness. I awoke slowly to the world and fell in love with it, for the first time all over again. I sat on my front porch watching neighbors' trees, recognized siblings in a web of life. A sense of belonging, ever elusive, was reemerging.

Transformation is not a pain-free process. What I was falling in love with—the natural world around me—was being lost at an alarming rate. There is a gravity and immediacy to the loss of planetary life. The same arrogance leading to the slaughters of Wounded Knee and of the American Indian came from a species arrogance that was threatening the planet I just remembered I loved.

———

The more I ran, the more I was able to run.

The more I ran, the better dressed I became. My wife encouraged my persistence, giving me an REI shirt technologically designed with underarm vent gussets and lamination-construction technology. Mostly, it was orange, and I thought I looked cool—a considerable upgrade from my PJ top. I quickly reached the pinnacle of running gear, purchasing something called "Coolmesh Wrightsocks," whose superior fabrics and technical features guaranteed pure comfort.

Finally, a client and I engaged in a brief discussion of best practices, where I learned of upgrading running shoes every two-hundred miles. I calculated three-hundred miles on my Boston Marathon Adidas, and determined it was certainly time to modernize. A second client shared that he regularly traveled fifty miles to Cheyenne to buy his running shoes at discount prices at Sierra Trading Post. I coerced an unwilling spouse to Wyoming, and emerged improved and sixty dollars impoverished, with a new pair of trail-ready Asics.

Change visited both running appearance and running experience. I ran longer distances. I transitioned from seven Old Town blocks to ten to Lee Martinez Park. The first week I gained entry to the park, I gasped and turned back. Then I inched deeper, struggling toward tall grass and trees. I felt a newfound closeness, imagined ageless secrets. My legs and lungs grew strong enough to carry me beyond civilization.

My head and heart expanded in preparedness. The iPod played as my body ran. Audible.com and Ishmael filled it with words. "You are captives of a civilizational system that compels you to go on destroying the world in order to live." "I'm telling you about living mythology not recorded in any book, recorded in the minds of people and being enacted all over the world." "We're not destroying the world because we're clumsy, we're destroying the world because we are in a very literal and disturbing way at war with it."

I reached the park's dividing line. On one side, the manicures of man. Here, I ran past tennis courts, picnic tables, swing sets and slides, across three basketball courts. Then, the grass transitioned from short and green to tall and untamed. Ishmael again, "This is what we need. Not just stopping things. … People need more than to be scolded. They need a vision of themselves and the world that inspires them."

———

Running (movement of body) and personal growth (movement of heart) collided. I arrived. The Poudre.

"This is the way of it. Let our story fires be lighted. Let our circle be strong and full of medicine. Hear me." Robbie Robertson on the iPod.

Right then I stopped running. I never ran again. Instead, I was talking to the long grasses as they passed, releasing trauma in steps, finding strength in a powder river. Robbie again, "This is rock medicine. The talking tree. The singing water. Listen. I am dancing underneath you."

The Poudre and Robbie, together now, "This is the way of it. It is a river. It is a chant. It is a medicine story."

Spring rains come. The river floods. I turn back prematurely, encounter pools I cannot cross. The Poudre is so full and happy. The summer sun starts, refuses to relent. The Poudre's anorexia begins. I want for rain, want for the Poudre to be strong and proud. Running alongside the Poudre, I care deeply. When our dialogue begins, I will learn the feelings are shared. A river, a chant, a medicine story, and now, a friendship.

———

As we ran side by side, I let the river in. My defensive walls of separation were disintegrating under the benevolent influence of this water deity. The Poudre was patient.

Slowly, I released the pain of a lonely past. Growing up alone, I taught myself there was no room for emotion. The world was not safe for feeling. Flashes from the past: Getting angry in the car, our old brown Chevrolet Malibu station wagon, Dad yelling that "anger is not acceptable." Crying silently. Then crying "too much," sent to my room, Dad angrily demanding with the classic "stop crying or you will really be given something to cry about." Second grade. I am so scared of feelings in particular, and adults in general, I don't dare ask the teacher on recess duty if I can use the bathroom. She was mean, and did mean things like take away my porcupine needles I brought for show and tell. She never gave them back. I secretly imagine they are in her home, displayed on some chest of drawers, her own private show and tell.

I secretly hoped to be found. I never imagined a river would find me. Thirty years after second grade, I still struggle to cry with people. The river gives me permission. Some days, I stop running. I am the man sobbing beside the river. I am the boy letting go of thirty years of unspoken pain. Growing up, surviving on the sparse diet of minimization and denial, I had little to sustain me. I'd thought a part of me starved to death. Today, the Poudre gives me permission to enjoy the rich taste of authentic expression. I am regaining my appetite for life.

Running the Poudre, I also mourned a lonely planet. The Poudre whispers: "You've been standing on a lie. You've believed in a dead world, unable to hear voices because dead things don't speak." And then, one day, a river speaks. "You believe a culture's great tragedy, that we are a collection of objects. Reclaim a Sacred Reality. We are a communion of subjects."

"Life is not an isolated experience. Things constantly shape one another."

A client tells me of his American Indian friend. He says, "All things are related. All things are related. All things are related." Then, "Don't let that white man in. It's a sacred ceremony." I think about what I've done in my past, of my relationships, based on repressed feelings and denied emotions, with self and with others; relationships based on domination, control, and, most of all, fear. Reading *Black Elk Speaks* helped me understand. I feel sad. I wouldn't let the white man in either.

Running the Poudre, I have a vision. I am standing by my tipi, safely nestled in the security of rock neighbors. There are two others, older like me. Outside, a benevolent valley welcomes two small children playing. They are laughing, dancing freckles floating in summer air. A breeze blows kisses at us all. It tickles. Then, blue gives way to dark grey, breeze to gusts. Quickly now comes a tornado. I am not able to reach the little ones. They are too far. I am safe in the shelter of stone. They are not. My heart sinks. Now I cry as I run (again). I know the metaphor—the tornado is an unformed awareness in the background of culture and life, an awareness that our world is being extensively damaged in each moment. The tornado's sudden coming is the industrial bubble bursting, possibly sooner than later; my pain, shock and tears, the ensuing trauma. I cannot reach the others because there is no collective solution that relies on the shelter of each other and our relationship with the earth.

Between the Poudre and me, there is hope. I tell the Poudre a little of what Ishmael shared on the iPod. The Poudre smiles, liking it. We come to an agreement. In a billion years, we will look back together. We will listen to the dolphins and the chimps and everyone else who is around at that time as they exclaim, "Man! Oh yes, man! What a wonderful creature! It was in his power to destroy the world and trample all our futures. But he pulled back and gave us all a chance. He showed us all how it is to be done if the world is to go on being a heaven forever. Man was the role model for us all."

I keep running, my powder river beside me. I am birthing into a world of increasing richness, increasing beauty. My river and I, we want to look back and smile. It may be a false hope. But it is ours. We cling to it.

# Highway Flagman
### John Calderazzo

*John Calderazzo teaches creative nonfiction writing at Colorado State
University. He is the author, most recently, of* Rising Fire: Volcanoes
and Our Inner Lives, *a book that looks at the many ways in which
volcanoes around the world have affected human culture. John was
stopped partway down the long-shadowed Poudre Canyon by a flagman, which gave him unexpected time to daydream. The result is
"Highway Flagman" which came to him as his mind kept traveling
even as the car slowed and stopped.*

This man about my age in a blaze
orange vest and wraparound shades
who has stopped me
three-quarters of the way
down Poudre Canyon,
what does he think about all day?

The tractor driver in braids
who's scooping rain-loosened rocks
from my lane?
The river below us pounding and twisting
between cracked, cubist walls?
The snowfields that yesterday
held the river?

He stands on the center stripe holding
his stop sign like a spear,
dreaming perhaps
of cutthroat trout, moose
browsing along Laramie River road,
Blue Paddle beer.

I sit in the car and wait,
tired from too much driving.
Late afternoon air slips
in the open window
and sifts over me
like the breath of a woman

I knew decades ago in Florida.

A scent of honeysuckle and oranges
fills the canyon,
and the high snows,
crusting over, withdraw
their fuel drop by drop
from infinitesimal engines
of gravity, though the river
crashing by does not yet feel this.

The two-lane road all shadow now,
the flagman's radio crackles,
and he leans in towards me,
saying, "Just stay in the oncoming."
I nod, as though he were merely
giving me directions.

# The Postcard
David Rozgonyi

*David Rozgonyi was born in 1976 in Tripoli, Libya, to Hungarian refugee parents. Travel and writing became a way of life as he back-packed across six continents, spending months among local residents in remote corners of the world. His first book of collected stories,* Goat Trees: Tales from the Other Side of the World, *was published in 2006. "The Postcard" is the result of a foray up Highway 14, and although this is a work of fiction, every word of it is true, somewhere along the Poudre River.*

Early on a summer afternoon, a postcard was delivered to a boxy white house in an outlying suburb of Fort Collins. The card was addressed to Aunt Marjorie Williams, 1220 Rake Street, and its front portrayed a mountain stream twisting through an alpine meadow while its back was filled with careful blue loops declaiming the dreamy thoughts of a young girl. *What a lovely trip this was, oh how many elk and fish and eagles there are up here, the wind is so cool and the river runs so fast!* The card ended with the exclamation—*In three days we leave! Please come visit me!* It was a charming card; the cards always were. Each time they arrived, sometimes two in one month, once nothing for almost a year, Mike Stutter, of 1220 Rake Street, dug them out of the trash after his wife threw them away.

"I wish they had a return address so I could tell the poor kid there's no Marjorie here!" Lori Stutter told her husband later that day. "Then again, maybe I wouldn't—they're always so sweet. She's always count-ing down the days to something. Three days till Camp Saguach. Six days until her school play. This time it was lunch at one o'clock; what was it last time? Her puppy's two-day birthday countdown? So precise!"

After smiling at the card as though it were a transparent glass beyond which, on the ground, sat the aforementioned puppy, Lori Stutter slipped it into the garbage beneath the kitchen sink. Mike Stutter waited until she went outside to water her window boxes. When the water came on, Mike plucked the card from the trash, examined it closely, put it in a shoebox in his closet, and joined his wife outside.

The day after the postcard came, the weather turned hotter; the day after that, hotter still. On the third day, not long after his wife left for work, Mike Stutter climbed behind the wheel of his ancient Datsun, started it up, and drove north, away from the city. When he got to Ted's Place, the general store on the corner of Highway 287 and Highway 14, he turned left.

Although Fort Collins grew like white fungus toward the mountains that hid just beyond these dry hogbacks, it had yet to invade this small prairie, and despite the breathless shimmering air, the view was uplifting. Leaving the larger road behind, shadows of vales were dotted with old plank structures trimmed out in white beneath isolated stands of oak. A wheel-turn sprinkler shimmered in a field on the north side of the road, beating water into air; on the south side, a mare hung her nose over a fence.

Mike let go of the wheel and wiped his forehead with his forearm as he approached the place on the horizon where the road dove out of sight between brown hills that grew up from the pasturelands like the folds in a rumpled blanket. It was hot, and the air coming through the open window was burning as Mike surveyed the hills; the power lines undulated beside the road, thick and purely black against the expanse of cornflower-colored sky, broken by smears of white with edges as sharp as marble patterns. But beneath that sky there was something else, for the moment betrayed only by a line of greenness and trees. In another minute, the river would meet the road, but for now it was slinking through the tall summer grasses, invisible until the last instant when both road and river would dive through the slot in the hills. A rise and fall in the land, then another, like the view from a plane on a windy takeoff roll, and then Mike entered the bottomlands of the Cache la Poudre, and the river was simply there.

There was no hurry. Highway 14 was a two-laner taking its time to rise, and Mike had hardly come above the level of the plains when he checked his watch and pulled into the first turnoff he found. He left his car and walked toward the waterline, gravelly and gentle, more like the banks of a beaver pond than any stretch of river; the river itself was wide and spent. He found shade and sat, enjoying cool pebbles beneath his jeans after the hot vinyl, and combing those that were between his splayed legs into circles and swirls with a knobby branch.

Briefly, his vision blurred and grew heavy. As night-shift supervisor at a small printshop in town, his mornings normally began much later than this. He rubbed his eyes and yawned. After very few hours of sleep, this morning he'd called in to take the night off—he knew from experience that he wouldn't be home for a while.

He threw the stick as far as he could. As he followed it downstream with his eyes, the motion of the water swam in his head—a whorl in two directions, the hand of an eddy the width of the river moving water first downhill beneath the truncated little cliffs, then uphill past the bank where he sat. The stick became trapped in the eye, bobbing amid small wavelets that peaked and fell, unsure as to where they should march, and Mike laughed. The Cache la Poudre, as beguiling and unlikely a name as Mike had ever heard, always managed to get him to do that, no matter how frequently over the past thirty years he made a trip to her shores.

As he sat, the sweat on his forehead lessened. The air was easier to breathe on the river, solid with vapor and the scents of trees, and the water gave it a touch of coolness that it did not possess on the eastern side of the hills. The scent of the river had the desired effect: It made him forget his home.

Rake Street in the middle of July; you could smell the shingles bake. The houses stood like simulacra, the original idea of tidy family homes perverted by the frenzied cloning emblematic of modern Colorado development. Featureless newborns, their lawns were green bedsheets only because the owners were fined one-hundred dollars if they let them go brown. There were no birds or squirrels—like some humans, these animals needed trees to be happy—and the scraggly aspens that were optimistically staked in a few of the yards weren't much help, destined as they were to die around the time the driveway started to sink and the colorful siding went to gray. Mike's white walls were cracking; his windows already leaked.

But ten minutes away from that, Mike found some relief as he leaned back on stiff arms. It was barely ten o'clock, and he sat dreaming on the shores of the river for a while, until there came the sounds of men hollering. Mike opened his eyes.

From around a bend, a gang of rafts floated into view, bearded young men laughing and clapping as they made landfall a hundred meters upriver. A van had eased behind Mike without his being aware of it, and when the doors slid open, two girls bounded out, grinning broadly and handing out drinks. They pulled the rafts up onto the shore, singing.

As Mike watched them, he saw in the lead boat a boy and a girl, both ten years old. The girl's brown hair was slicked and wet, the boy's shirt was soaked, but their faces were rapt. They vanished as the men leaped from the rafts, and Mike walked back to his car.

———

Highway 14 looped and meandered, following the course of the Cache la Poudre. Every so often, it branched off into small dirt drives or wooden bridges barely wide enough for a car beside clusters of mailboxes. Tiny alpine meadows slipped steeply into the water, and gravel berms broke small sidestreams away from the main flow, inches deep and rusty on the bottom, giving saplings purchase and minnows a place to rest. Houses dotted the wider banks, tucked in and smug, but Mike drove past all of these, slipping the car into turn upon turn, listening to the old, familiar springs creak beneath him and listing with the motion of the car until he felt like pulling over, and then he did.

He checked his watch—still only eleven—and walked to the river past trees filled with minute blue cicadas in the midst of frenzied mating, their hopeful, quintuple clicks like a thousand marbles knocking against one another. The river here was thinner and faster. Gone were the open, lazy pools, but the land wasn't yet steep enough to pinch the water into torrents and gyres, and Mike slipped his sandals by the black sandy shore.

Even in midsummer, the waters of the Poudre, like all mountain streams, could make you gasp. As Mike waded into the current, pain settled into his legs, insteps first but then driving inward along his nerves from there. Cold tendrils swept through the hair on his legs and drifting flecks of wood and sand scrabbled at his shins, but then, like all pain, it receded into something like the tickles of plants on his ankles, of which he was barely aware. Gravel massaged his toes as he splashed his arms and watched small ducks on the far bank dive the shallows for caddis larvae. A cloud stalled before the sun.

The water swirling around his legs washed away thoughts of his work, his wife, and everything else that had accumulated in the month since the last postcard had arrived. Mike faced upstream, and dreamed.

A noise like a small animal's cry startled him. It was an odd noise, one that might have come from his own distractions; it was the sound of a child crying out in joy. Over on the far bank, standing in a cove just shy of the faster moving current, were a young boy and his dad. They must have drifted down the edge of the current from past the bend upstream. Both of them were turned away so only their backs were visible, but it was enough to know they were bent low and together over the water, fiddling with something jumpy and flashing in the sunlight. Their poles—a long one for Dad, a kid-sized one for his son—flailed as the boy cried out again, excited, and Dad exclaimed something in the rumbling exclamations of dads.

The kid beamed at his dad, and Mike waded back to the shore, mildly surprised that his head was filled with thoughts of his father, and his feet were wrinkled and numb.

————

As Mike drove up Highway 14 and ascended into national forestland, the river turned gradually from a riffle-and-pool stream, twisting between pockets of meadow grass and stands of small trees, into a brave mountain stream filled with chutes and runs. He drove past a bend where kayakers practiced rolls in small hydraulics behind clean-swept boulders, past a place in the river where a slab of rock had burst from the cliffs above to pinch the river between its rocky fingers. He drove past a place where the bottom plunged and the water slackened into a crystal lens, fat and straining beneath fissured rocks cleaved by ice, beneath clouds building and collapsing, green flutes of rock tumbling into their own reflection, and past a hundred other places better even than these. All along now, Mike's shirt was dry. No matter the climate down where the ground flattened out, up in the mountains it was always cool and clear. Two minutes before one o'clock, Mike pulled from the road for the final time.

The overlook was a familiar place—one visit per postcard received, for almost twenty years now—so he stayed behind the wheel, all the windows down so the air flowed through. The road was high here, and it offered a view of the river below as it came around fins of rock, twisting first toward him and then away. Although it ran moderately here, something about the confluence of angles and summer air always made it seem as though there was only the sound of water, a noise like a ceaseless downpour, the backs of rocks like enormous turtles glistening far below in midstream.

Mike craned his neck to better see over the dash. The far side of the river was vertical or nearly so, but the near side opened to form a narrow meadow in the shape of a crescent moon, a green eddy of tall prairie grasses gone to seed, swirled through with purple and yellow. Gravel paths ran up and down the riverbanks in both directions beneath a line of reeds and whitebark saplings. Although the day was cool, and the burning city only thirty minutes away (had he not been dawdling and dreaming and wondering what would be asked of him today), the meadow was deserted but for a solitary blue sedan that glinted beneath the sky at the end of a small dirt lot.

A thin path dove from Highway 14 through a cut in a massive outcrop of rock, down toward the meadow below. Barely wide enough for one car, Mike eased his Datsun carefully between the rock walls. Once at the level of the river, he pulled beside the sedan and climbed from the car.

Mike crossed the crescent meadow slowly, keeping his eyes on the river. These bottomlands always carried the smell of his boyhood summer meadows—all fireweed and sky. It was the smell of fishing, playing, of all of his dreams running to the river hand in hand, and no matter the pressures of his marriage or his work, he forgot them all when he came here. And when he looked up and across the meadow, past clustering white butterflies lapping moisture from cracks in the ground, he saw an apparition in the shade of a rugged old mountain elm.

Tall, slight, and pressed toward the water by a brief gush of air down the sloped landscape, she looked insubstantial, an astral projection of the woman in the dreams Mike sometimes still had. The ponytail of dark hair that touched between her pale brown shoulder blades was more function than form, and she glowed against the fabric of her loose white sundress like amber. Her arms had the chiseled lines of a woman who was used to carrying dogs and holding infants in her arms; she held her simple sandals loosely in one hand.

A bird darted out of the tree that sheltered her and arrowed into the blue as Mike came to stand beside her. His voice was thick, but it was a familiar soft thickness brought about not by nervousness but by concern.

"Is everything okay?"

The woman smiled a little, and touched her cheek with the fingertips of her left hand. A gold ring reflected there, painful shards of glass in Mike's eyes. "Why shouldn't it be?"

"You look sad."

"I'm not anymore."

Mike looked across the field. A breath of wind cooled his forehead and made the willows moan. "Each year it's hotter down there. In the town."

"My husband upgraded the air conditioning last month," she said, shrugging. "I don't really notice it."

"I do. It's the worst at night."

"Open a window."

"My wife gets scared."

"Of what?"

"People."

"Burglars?"

"No, just people." Mike took a breath. "All I meant was that this is so much nicer. Up here."

"Much nicer."

The river swelled beside them as Mike watched it. "Lori liked your card."

The woman smiled again, but said nothing.

Mike nodded. "She said, 'if they ever came with a return address, we'd have to start answering them.' Eventually Marjorie's little niece will have to get a bit older."

The woman looked suddenly worried, and she turned to face Mike. "Has it been that long? Do you want me to stop?"

"No. We're not doing anything, are we?"

"No."

"What's the matter, then?"

The woman shook her head, not denying his question but deflecting it for the time being. "I fixed a little lunch, if you're hungry."

"Sure."

They started walking, down to the waterline, beside a stagger of white chevron-like eddies where the river caught on the rocks lying just beneath its surface; five paces farther, they sat where the water was glassy and bulbous. Trout sipped on the surface, little crescents that emerged beneath floating bugs, yawned, and then were gone.

The woman gave Mike a package wrapped in foil. He opened it. "I missed your sandwiches."

She smiled again. It was a pretty smile, one that was looking less tired now that they were out of sight of the meadow and the cars that reminded both of them that they would soon have to leave.

They ate together in silence, and then sat for a while in the sun.

"Do you remember when we came here with our parents?" Mike said at last. "That first time? We were ten, but this place is still the same. When I see you here, you're still ten, twelve, fourteen." He looked at his hands, the thick fingers and hair on the first knuckles, the scar on his thumb made by a blade many years ago but just past the diminutive knoll over the way, ten paces further on, in a hollow on the right, beside the rushing waters with this woman gasping beside him. "When you were sixteen. This river—" Mike followed scraps of trees caught in the current with his eyes, taking the old familiar lines downhill—"no matter what happens, this river can't change. So will you tell me what's the matter?"

Although there was never anything the matter—at least nothing that could be fixed by two people who knew better than to repeat the mistakes of history but couldn't allow their shared history to die—Mike could tell that she badly wanted to ask the things she always asked of him and tell him things that always tore him to hear. It was in the catch in her breath every now and again, and the way she was watching him, as though he were suddenly unfamiliar. In the end, she nodded. "Can we walk? Please, let's walk."

They stood amid the rattle of big, golden grasshoppers taking to panicked flight, and as they paced slowly down old trails they both knew well, the trees were bending around them, the ground humming beneath their shoes, and always the river, at every turn, every table, every vista, and the sound of water tumbling—a sound without beginning or end, the unbroken sigh of these dry hills. She was whispering, he was nodding, her shoulders shook, and the Cache la Poudre flowed around them as they remembered it to flow, washing out the world and everything else that had accreted between them over the years. Time sputtered and then stalled, but the river continued on for hours; when they returned to the meadow, the sun was almost out of the cup of the valley, and the shadows were running together. The air was cooling off, and they could smell the water as they paused in the shelter of a wispy alder.

"Why *do* you always come?" There was a depth in her voice as it fell away, the flicker of a plea.

"I've known you since we were eight," he said. "When we're a hundred, I'll still come. Every time you send me a card, I'll always come."

She smiled then, a faded smile as though she could all too easily recall the hollowness of her childhood, one that had been filled with old logs and empty rooms and twisty paths by dark brown rivers, until the man standing before her, then still only a fattish little boy with a brown John Denver bob and purple shorts, had moved in next door.

It was her turn to check her watch. "I should go."

"Ted will be worried."

She nodded. "So will Lori."

"I know. I should go."

"You should."

"I hate to worry her."

"I know. It's awful. I should go, too."

They stood for a moment listening to the river, and watching little tufted flies float like cottonwood puffs through dizzying depths of sky, trapped between the ground and the heavens, their wings caught in the last rays of the sun.

# PART 4

# Our Bodies Are Rivers

The human body is made up of two-thirds water, and so perhaps it is no surprise that we gravitate toward lakes and rivers. When we arrive at these oases, we use them for many purposes—to play, to think, to learn. The writers and poets in this section suggest that the Poudre River serves as a teacher. And we are taught many things—how to live, how to become more aware, and how to learn our place in a sustainable society. The contributors also seem to suggest that watery immersion teaches less tangible truths. Poet Lary Kleeman expresses it this way, "Restless, I am, for trying to see through things by way of explanation."

# Kingfisher
## Steve Miles

*Steve Miles is a high school teacher and lives in Denver with his wife, Teri, and kids, but makes frequent pilgrimages back to the Poudre and friends up north. His most recent publication is in* Comeback Wolves: Western Writers Welcome the Wolf Home. *Of this poem, Steve says, "It's thrilling to see the blue flash of a kingfisher diving into the river and emerging with a flashing piece of it. The pattern birds make in flight is river-like, and so sensual. The river was very quiet this day, and invited me to find the river in bird and self. I couldn't refuse."*
*This poem previously appeared in the* Southern Poetry Review.


This river knows
just where to touch itself.
The tongue of the river
& all its gleaming skin
has just now returned from the heart.

It renders before it holds,
slips before it knots
& all we see is the surface,
combed out like wind through wheat.

The spirit moved over
the face of the waters
exactly like a barn swallow—
gold & blueblack, quicker
than thought, creation pouring
from her keel.

A kingfisher rattles
into a dead tree. How many knots
will pass between us before we
unname one another?

A photograph of the river
tries to freeze this flux,
but death is an aperture
growing smaller, deepening
our depth-of-field.

When this river dies & rises
from her bed, who will inherit
the cobbled mattress?
Two jays upstream are happy
to bicker over it.

The river moves
deeper inside itself.
A stack of blank paper
with a pen on top.

Throw in a two-by-four
& watch it flop
over fluid swells,
elusive hips.

Kingfisher says,
Why feel wooden inside love?

Our bodies are rivers, thirsty
for more of us.
If you want to catch something,
dive from the sun.

# Surfing the River
### Todd Mitchell

*Todd Mitchell lives with his wife, Kerri, in Fort Collins, Colorado. He has kayaked for ten years and has spent countless hours on the Poudre River. He currently teaches writing at Colorado State University. His first novel,* The Traitor King, *will be published by Scholastic in 2007.*

T he river troll lives beneath the cow grate that crosses Highway 14 at the mouth of Poudre Canyon. He pokes his hands through the bars. Driving to the put-in from Fort Collins, I honk, so I don't run over the troll's fingers and incur his wrath on the river. Most other kayakers I know do this too.

About a half mile before reaching Poudre Park, I pull off the side of the road to take a look at "the rock"—a large, triangular-faced boulder with orange numbers painted on it. For boaters, this is Mecca. In the early spring, we drive up the canyon and eagerly e-mail each other about how high the river might get. When the water reaches "1" on the rock, there are a few secret waves that it's possible to surf. When it reaches "1.5" the river is bony, but high enough that you can scrape your way down some sections. At "2" you can kayak most areas, play in friendly holes, catch eddies, and practice strokes. At "3" the river's fully alive. At "4," it's a whole new river—most of the rocks that were visible throughout the rest of the year are covered, waves are so high that you can't see what's ahead, and some holes could suck your boat down and pin you to the bottom. Anything above "4" and the river becomes a frantic, wild ride, with chest-thumping water, and current so powerful it can make simple maneuvers, like ferrying from one shore to the other, extremely difficult.

The river's just above "4.5" today—the highest I've seen it in years.

I turn off Highway 14 a few hundred feet above the rock at the Pineview Falls put-in. Kerri, my wife, decides she'd rather put in below this section, where it's mostly class III and IV water. Pineview is a short

IV+ rapid at this level. There are other difficult sections further up river, but most boaters don't run those when the water is this high.

Kerri takes the car keys and kisses me good-bye. I'm busy tightening some straps on my gear. She gives me a half-angry, half-concerned look.

"You shouldn't go alone," she says.

"I'll be fine. I've done this part dozens of times before."

Kerri frowns. She knows I've never done it at this level. And I know she's right—it's not smart to boat alone. But it's such a perfect spring day, and the section is short, and for some reason I can't turn back now that I'm here.

"If you break your neck, don't expect me to push your wheelchair," she says.

I kiss her again, then carry my boat down to the water.

———

Last summer, after paddling a section of the Taylor River near Gunnison, Colorado, I hitched a ride back to my car with two other kayakers from Oregon. The driver, Ben, was a rising kayak rodeo star, and his copilot, Josh, was a world-class creek boater, until he dislocated his shoulder paddling in Chile (the river he was on ran through a steep gorge, so he had to continue paddling for the rest of the day, dislocating his shoulder several more times on the way down and doing permanent damage).

Ben had decided to move to Colorado. The back seat of his car was packed full of clothes and a stereo that kept falling on me at every left turn.

"How were the rivers in Oregon?" I asked, feeling obliged to start a conversation—once I hitched a ride in Alaska with a woman who told me she only expected psycho killers to be silent.

"Awesome," said Ben. "Especially around Ashland. The creeking season is far better than anything I've found out here."

"Isn't that where Roberts died?" asked Josh.

"Which one?" asked Ben.

"The oldest brother."

"Yeah," said Ben. "I think he died on Rip creek. I used to paddle with David, the youngest brother. He just died on the Rogue."

"God, they were awesome playboaters."

"They both died on class IV water," said Ben, shaking his head because they were paddlers who regularly boated class V creeks. "Both brothers breached against a rock and their boats folded around them."

We rounded a corner and Ben honked at some cows standing glassy-eyed in the road.

"Same thing happened to Jackson," said Josh. "We were up on the Arkansas, had run the Numbers and were going to set up camp for the night. Jackson wanted to do one more rapid, so he went off alone. It was simple water, but he fell against a rock that was cut away beneath the surface, flipped, and got wedged under there."

"That happened to a guy on the Poudre," I said. "It took the rescue workers days to get the body out. I think they had to lower the river level."

Josh and Ben nodded, then continued to talk about paddlers they'd known who'd died or been injured. The odd thing was that so many of the expert boaters they mentioned had accidents on class III and IV water, as if the greatest danger lay in thinking things were easy.

———

On the Poudre River there are features named Killer Bridge (where someone seems to die every four or five years), Decapitation Rapid (so-called because of the way the current sucks you toward a spike jutting out of a bridge pylon at head height), and Cardiac Corner (a blind turn where the water funnels, launching you straight toward a knife-edge rock). The names are reminders of how deadly the river can be. But also, they're something else—a celebration, maybe, of the danger that's part of the sport.

Shark attacks and river deaths always seem to make front page news. Never mind that it's far more likely we'll die from the vehicles we drive, or the food we eat, or the pollution we breathe. We're a culture obsessed with the few violent deaths, rather than the pervasive, ordinary ones. And always there's that question: Why do people choose to put themselves at risk?

Why do I?

The funny thing is, I'm one of the most cautious, fearful people I know. Last weekend, I freaked out about the dust from the mulch I shoveled in my back yard, afraid that it would cause a fungus to grow in my lungs and suffocate me. I fear mercury in the water, asbestos drifting down, and radon gas floating up. I fear that every freckle I see on my skin is cancer. I fear nuclear war. I fear a sudden heart attack. I fear a drunk trucker plowing into me on the highway. I fear stray bullets from my crazy neighbor. I fear slowly being poisoned by some chemical I'm unaware of. I fear the invisible, meddling things, and the big, senseless things. I fear that thinking about my fears might cause them to happen.

Basically, I fear what I can't control, and this is why I go kayaking.

————

The water today is so high that it laps above the bottom step of the put-in. I balance my kayak against a tree root, slide my legs in, lock my knees against the hull, then pull the skirt over the cockpit, sealing myself in. It's a tight fit.

One of the first things I learned when I started paddling over a decade ago is that kayakers don't name their boats. You might name a sailboat, or a canoe even, but not a kayak, because a kayak is more like a pair of pants you put on. You can't afford to think of it as something separate from yourself. It's the clothing you wear to become part of the current.

I tip myself off the tree root and into the water. Usually, there's an eddy near the shore, where the current cycles backward, flowing upstream, but with the river this high the eddy is blown out. Immediately, the water pushes the bow of my boat, turning me downstream. I give a few sweep strokes, then paddle hard against the current to keep from getting drawn too far down as I ferry across the river. The current's faster than I'd thought. In no time, my arms are aching and my heart is racing. Across the river, I barely catch the back end of an eddy and paddle up, taking shelter behind a large rock.

Then I dart back into the current. The river folds around the rock, creating simmering white whirlpools that I throw the edge of my boat into, momentarily sinking the bow under and doing cartwheels. Playboaters sometimes come to spots like this, using the waves and holes formed by the current to initiate blunts, pinwheels, and aerial loops—surreal water gymnastics that don't seem possible until you see them performed. But I'm too nervous about what lies downriver to spend much time playing.

Again, I eddy out and rest, and then I paddle through the rapid. The boulders I normally use to mark my descent are mostly covered. A few waves thump my chest, splashing my face with water. I catch an eddy behind the "number" rock. From here, I can pause and scout the next section before continuing on.

Pineview Falls is a narrow chute formed by two house-sized boulders, where the water cascades over jagged rocks. To paddle it safely, I need to skirt a large hole, turn in an eddy, ferry back, then paddle into the current near the boulder on river-left that will take me down the falls. I make the first set of moves fine, but as I'm crossing the mouth of the falls, I misjudge the size of a wave. The bow of my boat shoots into the air. For a moment, it hovers there and I fight for balance. Then the water flips me backward, and I'm upside down, being sucked toward the falls.

The ice cold water grips me. Time slows. Bubbles hold before my eyes, glittering silver. If I slip over the falls upside down, there's a good chance my head will be slammed against a rock. I picture the rock rushing toward my face, a sudden bone-crunching smack, then my body being carried, unconscious, down river. It's too late to go back or try again. I can't reason with the river or charm my way out of this. The water will keep flowing with no pause for my death.

There's a recurring dream I have in which I'm kayaking in the ocean when a huge wave rises in the distance, blocking out the sun. The wave builds and builds, its tremendous undertow sucking me toward it. Water glows bright blue as sunlight streams through the wave's peak, outlining the silhouettes of fish and sharks beneath the surface. Then the crest arcs over and curls into a huge white claw. For a moment, I'm paralyzed with fear—helpless in the shadow of forces beyond my control. I know that if the wave breaks, I'll drown before I ever find the surface.

And this is how kayaking in rivers has changed my sense of fear—in my dream, I swim with the wave, and just as my terror peaks, threatening to crush me, I surf the huge dream-wave. I slide down the water's face, unafraid.

I find that stillness now as I drift upside down toward the falls. I arc my body and roll up. It's too late to paddle away. All the water in the river is channeled through this spot, creating a flow far too powerful to fight against. And I don't have to. I stick my paddle in, feel the river tremble against the paddle's face, and move myself straight into the current. The water carries me smoothly over the falls.

I rest in the pool below. Looking back, I study the tumultuous white braiding of currents more complicated than I can comprehend. Then I continue on, drifting with the river, learning to be part of something larger than myself.

# Sudden Swim (with apologies to Robert Service)

Scott Woods

*Scott Woods is an engineer living in the foothills west of Fort Collins. His love of the outdoors has been expressed through years spent rock climbing, kayaking, and just hanging out. This poem was written after an unpleasant high-water swim through the "white mile" section on Upper Rustic. This run remains one of his favorite stretches of river.*

There are strange things done in pursuit of fun
By those who float down creeks,
Whether chancing a roll in a boiling hole,
Or paddling easy sneaks.
The folks on the banks may offer thanks
That they're not the ones imperiled.
But the guys who squirt, and who often flirt
With death, are the ones who get barreled.

On a warm summer day we were floating our way
In our boats which have no sail,
When the water rose to humongous flows,
And we all turned awfully pale.
The river crashed, and I got trashed
As it pushed up against a rock.
I tried to roll, but lost control,
Then I swam with a sudden shock.

And now I dream of how long in that stream
I struggled with waves crashing down.
I couldn't breathe, and the wild water seethed—
For a while I feared I would drown.
The waves just soared, and the water roared—
Way too much found its way down my throat.
I was saying a prayer from out of despair,
When at last my hand grabbed a boat,

And my bud was there, and he gave me a stare
That helped me to ignore the cold.
So I put on a face to hide my disgrace,
As slowly to shore I got towed.
I was cold, I was wet, and I had one regret—
That my roll and brace had betrayed me.
But I swore I'd be back, for another attack
On this run which attempted to slay me.

# A Subtle Doubt

## Ian Ellis

*Ian Ellis is currently studying at Prescott College in Arizona, though he grew up a mile away from the Poudre River. The banks of the Cache are his place to escape, meditate, ponder, and reflect, and these words were born while sitting next to the river and contemplating the proposed Glade Reservoir.*

I never knew
it was so deep.
Silence bores me down her stream
as I recline
until the selfless waters engulf.
What was I?
Prying eyes can't reveal
wanton believers only try
Arrogance lost in the clouds
—sparse and far apart
but a soft, radiant white.
A tear for a raindrop.

# Stations

Blair Oliver

*Blair Oliver teaches literature and creative writing at Front Range Community College in Fort Collins, where he's also the founding editor of* Front Range Review. *He has published numerous stories in periodicals and anthologies, and has a regular outdoors column in* Yellowstone Journal. *About his story, "Stations," Blair says, "Trout and their waters don't need us. It's we who need them. A river was something the men in my family could agree on, and because of that, it became the thing we couldn't share. Fishing, like a story, is an exercise in hope, even when the rest of life isn't."*

The last time I saw my father he carried in his pack a half-gallon bottle of Smirnoff's vodka and a jar of cocktail onions. He dropped his rod case and set the booze and onions on the card table my wife and I had placed outside our tent in Poudre canyon. The table was my idea, as was the family-sized tent, lawn chairs, and the decision to car camp in case Jody, who'd wanted to hike into the wilderness, went into early labor. She was still twelve weeks from giving birth, but I insisted, like I did about the cup of milk a day and the vitamins. Insufferable, I know. Jody retaliated by inviting my father to join us without telling me. She left camp for a walk before he'd pulled in.

Stunned, I watched him as I propped my rod against the tent. My father, a railroad engineer, shook my hand then started looking around for glasses.

"The olives are hatching," I lied, hitching the strap on my waders. "Let's go down to the river first."

He turned from the cooler. His thin, graying hair was greasy, as was his forehead, and his eyes were bleary and red from the thousand-mile drive. The neck of the T-shirt beneath his flannel was yellow with sweat.

"I'm still bigger than you," he said.

"What?"

"You wouldn't want to mess with me."

I looked at him to see if he was already drunk. His hand shook as he kept it, slightly cupped, against his trousers. It was hard to see the person before me as the man I once spent a holiday with on the train, seated on his lap in the engine, rolling through the endless plains of Nebraska where the wheat waved like little golden soldiers.

"No, Sir," I said, addressing him like I used to.

"Very well then." He threw back a shoulder as if to crack it, then reached into the cooler. "Let's have a drink."

I'd always been afraid of my father. Maybe I still was, but for the first time I felt sorry for him. Did it ever end? It wasn't a physical fear at this point, although he was, as he said, bigger than me.

"I'll pour the drinks," I said, taking the Dixie cups from him.

He leaned his pack on a pine and lowered himself against it. Tourist traffic drowned out the river, which was low from drought. My father's eyes searched up through the trees at the steep canyon wall bearded with lichen. Our fellow campers blared their boom boxes, chased their dogs.

"Do you have plastic swords for the onions?" my father asked.

"Are you challenging me to a duel?"

He frowned. "I'm just kidding, you know that," he said. My father peered into his cup before sipping. Then he shrugged his right shoulder, which was higher than his left so that he often looked like he was leaning that way, and took another sip as I lowered my waders and sat in one of the lawn chairs across the fire pit from him.

"So how was the drive?" I said.

"It rained in Iowa."

As a teacher, I was a fine lecturer, but I was generally no good one-on-one. Part of me had hoped Jody was pregnant with twins so I wouldn't ever have to be alone with my only child. I was afraid I'd botch all of those man-to-man talks with a son.

"Did you stop anywhere?" I asked my father.

"Yeah," he said, "the Corn Palace." He screwed up his mouth and motioned for me to bring him the bottle. I did. "What kind of a question is that?"

"An ordinary one. The kind people ask when visitors arrive."

He poured another drink as I sat again. The bottle was on the ground between us.

"Where did you eat?" I started back out of my chair. It tipped to the ground. The gesture would've been effective if I was angry, but I wasn't. "Would you like something to eat?" I said, righting the chair.

He held out his hand to stay me. "I'm fine, Jimmy."

We were quiet for a few moments. I hadn't been called Jimmy since the first time we'd fished together, ten years earlier. Even though he was an expert with access to private waters, my father had never taken me fishing when I was a kid. Flyfishing, for him, was a thing apart from the rest of his life, even though my mother and I were never a big part of that either. He'd only taken me to his honey hole when I showed up on his doorstep with my new rod and demanded he teach me. It wasn't too late for us, I hoped.

Clouds were banking above us in the canyon, darkening it, and I started to think the mayflies might really be coming off by then. We looked at each other over the tops of our cups.

"I would've made better time, but it was raining," he said. "It follows me."

"That'll help with the trout."

"Then there was the construction."

This was good. This was better. This was what polite conversation was supposed to sound like. We finished our drinks and made a couple more. My father seemed to sit straighter against his pack as I slunk a little, feeling the warmth of the booze. Ten years earlier, he'd positioned me at the tail of a pool that stacked up behind a trio of half-submerged boulders. Pale Morning Duns were lifting from the film, and here and there we heard, then saw, spirited rises. My emerger drifted in the film at the back of the pool as my father stood alongside me, pinched his rod in his armpit and watched.

He'd said that the pool was where the trout should've been, even if they weren't. After a few rough casts, my line throbbed and came up taut. I thought the fish had hooked itself. I moved to get it on the reel, mistakenly lowered my tip, and the line went limp. My father put his hand on my shoulder and told me to try again. Moments later, my leader butt stuttered in the center of the pool. I set the hook. The fish made a smart, little run before I eased it to my father's net. "A man can take your wife or your money," my father had said, gently moving the small brown back and forth in the water, "but he can't take this." I didn't know if he'd meant our relationship or the fish. We'd only seen each other a few times between then and now. When we did, though, we fished on the Poudre River, and there at least, it was never awkward.

He looked around us at the crowded campground, presumably for Jody, though he didn't ask after her. I didn't think he knew that the invitation wasn't from both of us. In the past, I'd disappointed my father with my inability to keep up with his drinking and my propensity for what he called bookish thoughts instead of practical knowledge. With the baby coming, I wasn't interested in thirteenth-hour parenting tips from wise fools. Now, he asked if I'd talked to my mother recently.

"Sure," I said, warily.

"You know I'm a happily married man, don't you?"

"Sure. Deb's great." My father's wife and I had only met once. She laughed after every sentence she spoke, meaty breasts heaving, so I wasn't sure what she thought about anything. She'd read my palm and told me my life line left something to be desired.

"I've been dreaming about your mother again," he said, looking at me significantly over his cup.

"You're not going to tell me about it, are you?"

"I'll never love another woman like your mother," he said. "But she closed her legs to me. Do you understand?"

He meant my mother caught him sleeping with waitresses, bar girls, and housekeepers along his line and didn't immediately forgive him. His real drinking began then, but he never made an excuse about that.

"Look," I said, "I'm not sure I'm comfortable talking about this."

"I'm a happily married man," he said.

I poured myself another drink. I thought Jody should be back soon from her walk downstream. She wouldn't want to find us like this, but she'd sowed it. She meant well, of course. While I tried to ignore problems, Jody tried to solve them. She didn't know any other way to get my father and me to talk again before the baby was born but along the river.

"I went to Ellis Island," he said when I sat again, resting my cup on a thigh patch.

"Oh yeah? Sounds like fun." The alcohol was no help here. I steeled myself for a story about Ireland, "the homeland," as my father sometimes called it.

"I found your great-grandfather's name: 'James McTavosh, 1901.'"

"Good. Good."

"Jamie Mac came over here with his brothers, three of them, all three with nothing, and ended up with the largest pipe-laying outfit in the state. I worked for my grandfather when I was a boy."

This, I thought, was an accusation.

"One time my grandfather—this was when I first started working for him—sent me back from the jobsite to the yard to pick up something he'd forgotten."

"What was it?" I interrupted.

"That's not important right now, son. Listen. You might learn something today, professor."

I took a drink.

"I didn't have a driver's license yet," my father said. "I was fourteen, but he gave me his new Chevrolet to take back to the yard. No, I didn't crash the truck. Listen to me. I drove to the yard and talked to a few of the men there, used the bathroom and so on, then got back into the truck and returned to the site. I don't think I even rolled down the window. My grandfather greeted me and asked for the part. I'd completely forgotten. I had to tell him that. I drove to the yard and back without realizing I'd forgotten the part or even remembering why I went."

"Strange," I said.

"I can still see the disgust on the old man's face."

"You have to admit it's funny," I said.

"That incident has shaped my life."

I waited for him to tell me how.

"That old man became a millionaire. But you know what? He wouldn't spend a goddamned dime. Made his wife live in a barn. Later, he paid cash for a house for my father. My father was an asshole when it came to business, but that's another story. That's the story about why we no longer have the company, why you and I never got to work together, why we're not better friends."

I opened my mouth, but no words came. I could only wonder what working together might have been like. We could've been like those fellows you sometimes saw sitting alongside each other in a pickup, sipping coffee out of thermoses and laughing as they rubbed their hands against the cold. Would I have a joke to tell him? I'd have taken the chance, I now thought, surprising myself.

"Anyway, after hoarding his money for so many years, the old man finally bought his wife a new house and a car and even joined the local fishing and hunting club, where he thought he'd take up sport. Two weeks later—I'm talking fourteen days—he died of an aneurysm."

"Goes to show you," I said, lamely.

"Meanwhile, his brother Colm, your great uncle, spent and drank and fished every day of his life. He lived to be ninety-three, high times, my man, until the end."

My father's story was a long one for such an obvious conclusion. Maybe he'd read something like it in *Reader's Digest* and was now confusing it with our family. He'd had all of his life to work on the story, and it should've ended sooner. Maybe it was my fault it hadn't ended at the part in which we were friends. Words were failing us here.

"That's frightening," I said, "to die just like that. Maybe it would be better to get sick for—"

"I like to drink," my father said. "I'm going to keep drinking because that's one of the few things I still like to do."

Night was falling. Here and there, camp stoves flared in the dusk. Jody was a climber, with considerable orienteering skills, so it only took me several martinis to not worry about her extended walk. She was giving us time. We drank quietly for a while, occasionally ducking errant Frisbees. Every few minutes my father would mumble something, smile, or frown as if he were by himself, then look back up at me, surprise creasing his sweaty brow.

"Are you getting hungry yet, Dad?" I finally said. "We should eat something."

"You go ahead," he said. "I'm fine."

There wasn't much in the cooler. Though I didn't usually keep the fish I caught, I'd planned on killing a few for dinner. My father's back was to me against the tree. His cup was almost empty again.

"We better go fishing," I said, standing before him.

He raised his eyebrows. "You're all right, professor, you know that?"

I couldn't tell if he was making fun of me.

"You know I'm proud of you, don't you?"

I felt silly about how that warmed me inside. Then I sat as a wave of guilt washed over me about what I'd been thinking of him.

"That's okay," he said. "I want all of this for you. Your big house. Jody. Your degrees and your job. What father wouldn't? Every man should be lucky enough to be an embarrassment to his son."

"Is that what you think? That I'm ashamed of you?"

"You know I killed a man not long ago," he said.

"Excuse me?" I almost hollered.

"Jody knows this," he said. "That's why she invited me here without you knowing."

I lowered my drink. "Slow down," I said.

"He jumped in front of my train."

"Oh. Then you didn't—"

He shook his head, then snapped his shoulder. "Tell that to the man's family. He wasn't a suicide, they said."

"Of course he was a suicide. It's not like you turned into him. It's not like you could've stopped short in front of him."

"I couldn't?"

"No."

He rose from the ground and braced his cup-hand against the tree. His knuckles flushed. My father's hands were large and lumpy as lunch bags full of rocks.

"It really shook me up," he said. "I started drinking again. Seriously drinking. The company made me go to a counselor after I saw something cross the tracks in front of me a few weeks later. Maybe they were right. Maybe it was just a deer." He shook his head, remembering. "I started seeing things that weren't there. I stopped the train, Jimmy. I shut her down in the middle of nowhere."

"Did they force you out?" I asked.

"No," he said. "They wouldn't do that. They're not like that. They're decent people, most of them."

We drank in silence. What else didn't I know about my father?

"When is that wife of yours getting here?" he asked.

It was dark, and we still hadn't left camp.

"Soon," I said.

"You better find her."

I left for the woods, pausing only to grab my rod in case I found Jody sitting comfortably on a rock, in no hurry, along a run boiling with trout. Raising my waders as I walked, I reached the river and headed downstream. The noise of the campground was lost in moving water. Here, the woods cleared, and the night was drilled with stars. My mouth was dry. I seemed to go right from drinking to the hangover.

Rings shimmered in a pool. Above it, spinners swirled. I stopped and watched as three large trout rose rhythmically, sipping bugs like supplicants receiving communion. Bats buzzed. I couldn't see Jody ahead of me on the trail. She wouldn't know I was looking for her. If anyone was going to get lost in the woods, it was me. Maybe my father would catch up if I waited for a cast or two.

I pulled line from my reel and roll-cast up and across, thirty feet, to the head of the pool. One upstream mend, and the fly scooted into the first fish's lane. I knew this without seeing it. I tracked my tip where the fly ought to be.

Once upon a time I kept a black-and-white picture of my father in my office. He was tall, sinewy, standing bare-chested along the South Fork with a bamboo rod and a can of beer. His chest was a bit sunken, and his jeans fell below his thin hips. He wore his hair short with the longish sideburns that were fashionable at the time. The photographer, one of his buddies I imagined, for that was what he'd be called, must've known what he was doing. The canopy of trees above my father bowed in the same way he was standing so that he was very much a part of the scene, as much as the moving water, the rocks, and the woods itself. This was composition. In my entire life, I had never felt as at-ease, as graceful even, as my father looked in that picture. More than once a colleague or a student had stood before the picture and asked me where I liked to fish, did I use dry flies or wet, and I'd had to explain how that wasn't me along the river, that I wasn't a very good fisherman, that my father and I didn't even look much alike anymore.

The trout rose and I raised my rod. I let him run.

———

When I got back to camp, my father was on his knees, hunched over a section of model railroad. In the lantern light next to him, seated with her legs folded under her, was my wife. They'd laid a dozen feet of track and had the engine and the cars on a curve, heading into a toy town and station, with themselves in the center. Beside them were my father's empty pack, two cups and the bottle. Jody's cup, I imagined, held barely a sip. Their shadows bled on the pine needles. From the dark at the edge of camp, I thought they looked like a boy and girl at Christmas, but ones who needed to be held, protected, as if they weren't used to such riches and might grow frightened at my slightest sound. Or maybe that was just my father. Jody was radiant, her thick red hair gathered loosely over her shoulder. She raised her cup and held it on her pregnant stomach.

I stared at the high, clean walls of our new tent, the lantern and the card table, the chairs, the fishing tackle there, and felt like a stranger, an awkward intruder in some other man's life. My good fortune embarrassed me. Jody's cup had a hint of lipstick on the rim.

She must have heard me breathing.

"For the baby," she said, craning up to see me. "Isn't that sweet?"

"Right here," I thought I heard my father mumble. "It happened right about here."

I came into camp, and Jody moved a little to give me room. I sat beside them and placed the fish before my father.

Before there were words, there was water. It was the oldest sound. It was the sound we always came back to. Jody put her hand over mine. My father laid another section of track before looking at the rainbow in the needles, the last fish, I suddenly knew, he'd ever see. He raised his glass. With it in his hand were a toy couple and a baby. I watched as they rose toward his mouth, then took a drink, waiting for his hand to fall.

# Watercolor
## Lary Kleeman

*Born and raised in Colorado, Lary Kleeman has taught high school English since 1992. A graduate of Colorado State University and of the MFA program at the University of Montana, Kleeman is a recipient of the Colorado Council on the Arts Poetry Fellowship. It was a glorious October afternoon when he and his wife were at the river's edge. She was doing a plein air painting of the river and its trees, and he was inspired to write this poem.*

Restless, I am, for trying to see

        through things by way of

explanation.

     We watch the Poudre slide by.

A water ouzel tattoos the air

        with its wrenny song.

Dumbly caught in the severity of pose,

           rocks gray to

the reticence

they live.

You ask how could blue be so blue

as sky enters clean, spare, autumnal.

        I answer in terms of
aridity.

    (When will I awaken?)

On course for the uncharted,

       the world goes

without

saying.

# Ashes
## Kathleen Dean

*Kathleen Dean is a writer in Fort Collins, Colorado, where she enjoys the Poudre River with her husband and three children. She appreciates the way the Poudre winds its way through her life during times of both happiness and loss. She wrote this story as her thanks to the river for its presence throughout these times.*

We're winding our way up the Poudre Canyon in my old 4 x 4—a strange group, to be sure. There's me at the wheel, hoping this morning will go right. There's my 14-year-old son, silent in the backseat, watching the canyon flash by. There's dark-eyed Eva, whom my son and I don't really know. And there's the dead woman, Mary, friend of my son and Eva. Eva guards Mary's cremated ashes at her feet in a bag of crushed velvet. Mary wanted her ashes scattered in the river up this canyon, and we are on our way to honor her wish.

I glance at my son in the rearview mirror. His hair is still damp from his early morning run. He'd tugged self-consciously at his running clothes when I picked him up from cross-country practice. "Shouldn't I change?" he'd asked. "I mean, since …" he'd trailed off. His green eyes shone bright for a moment. Mary wouldn't mind what he wore, I'd told him. She'd just be glad he came.

Mary died months ago, a suicide. I reeled when I got the news—such a final decision and an abrupt departure for someone who'd stuck out life for more than sixty years. Many things had gone wrong for Mary; I knew there'd been chronic illness, debilitating bone pain, family estrangements. But she had remained active and—I had thought—engaged in living. Just days before her death, we'd planned meals for a sick friend together, and she'd told me about the deer and eagles she watched in the foothills around her home. I hadn't seen this death coming, and I didn't understand it.

It was worse for my son, who shared a kindred-spirit friendship with her for years. When I told him she was gone, he had paled, then nodded his head in one short jerk as if to say, *So that's how it is,* and clammed up.

Knowing my son was something that had gone right for Mary. The friendship that started when he was a grade-schooler in bifocals and she was a silver-haired artist near retirement had gone right for *both* of them. They often walked and talked along the neighborhood irrigation canal diverted from the Poudre River. One summer day when my son was younger, I joined them. They had crunched along through dried grass, heads up, searching for ripe mulberries. Mary spotted a cluster of sunflowers. She rushed ahead to stand shoulder-to-shoulder with them and finger their silky petals. She blew pollen from her palm. "They're *beautiful*," she said. Her tone bordered on complaint that we'd only just today stumbled across them, that we'd missed out up to now.

She and my son talked as they walked on ahead. She promised to bring him her next copy of *Architectural Digest.* She asked how his artwork was progressing, considered his ideas about religion and shared her own, and agreed that yes, sometimes kids could be mean.

Now that he's older, my son knows what to talk about and not talk about with his classmates—yes to personal records for the 5K or weekend plans, no to histories of clipper ships, Civil War trivia, or an analysis of the architectural styles that contributed to Victorian design. He has shed his glasses now, shot up several inches, added muscle to his thin frame, and learned what it feels like to belong. But there had been a time when Mary's friendship offered him a life raft.

In return, he had offered her, perhaps, the happiness of a relationship with a son or grandson without the complications. After she died, my son and I learned that she had kept everything he ever made her: a galley ship made from a yucca pod, a Victorian-style house design, pencil sketches, more. She displayed them in her home alongside the professional works of her fellow artists.

Because I am deeply grateful for their friendship and because I am haunted by the image of Mary dying alone, I hope for a lot today. I want our actions to take care of her in a way that no one could while she lived—and in turn take care of myself, my son, and Eva.

I met Eva for the first time at the memorial service, which Eva had arranged. She was my age or younger; she and Mary had been best friends. Eva said she planned to scatter Mary's ashes on the Poudre when the time was right. She said of course we could come along.

Now that we've come, I'm feeling awkward. We have no minister, no script, and no experience in scattering ashes. I feel as if we must make something from nothing. We've grown quiet in the truck, perhaps all wondering how this will work out. But we've made our way up to the spot that Eva has chosen, and there's nothing for it but to pull in and park.

We unload our cargo: a book about rivers, pen and paper, sage, matches, Mary's box in its velvet bag. Then we stand with arms full and look around. It's a happy place, an open area where families come to enjoy the water. The river is running high, talking to itself as it rushes by. The leaves on the cottonwoods are already glowing yellow, and the air has an autumn chill.

How right that the sky is muted today instead of its usual, northern Colorado bright-eyed blue. How right everything around us feels, in fact. The river seems in charge up here. My awkwardness slips away.

Eva holds out the velvet bag. "Do you want to choose the spot?" she asks my son. Her offer takes my breath—a gift. He looks across the river, then back at us. "Yes, I do," he says. He accepts the bag and holds it in both arms.

And so my son leads the way, and we pick our steps among water-worn rocks on the edge of the Poudre. He stops by a set of flat stones that lead into the water. Eva pulls Mary's crematory box from the bag, pries open the lid, and hands my son a bag of creamy colored, finely powdered ashes.

On the rocks in the Poudre, we say our goodbyes. We write private messages. Burn sage. Speak aloud. Eva and I speak many words; my son simply tells Mary that he will miss her. And this is enough. The three of us exchange clear-eyed glances. "Are you ready?" Eva asks my son. He climbs onto the rock in the middle of the current, opens the bag, and begins to gently shake its mouth over the clear water.

# Maenad
### Evan Oakley

*Evan Oakley teaches at Aims Community College in Greeley, Colorado. His poetry has appeared in many publications including* North American Review *and other anthologies. For many years, he codirected Loveland Colorado's annual "Poets in the Park" festival, which featured many nationally famous poets. In his poem below, Evan discusses the diversity of people that find refuge in and along the Poudre.*

The laundromat was warm, full
of buttery light in the snowstorm;
the religious tracts were there,
promises of heaven, where white
and black children lay down with lions,
their singing contending with the nose-bleed
staccatos staining the dryer lids.

The frugal tribes, and the displaced were there,
observing the orisons of their kind,
and since it was the evening the many-coated
women had arrived, come out of the foothills
in trucks, come down off Storm, come from up
the Poudre, to do the once a month washing.
Their tanned faces and blue eyes were the color
of unimaginable reveries. They were artisans
because they could string a bead; they were
a quarter Cheyenne because they had dreamed it;
they believed that the gravel in their lockets
could focus the cosmic body of god.

One had a truckbed where geese rode in cages,
feathers white as the snow piling in drifts
around them, and in the cab a spotted hound
licked the sticky mouths of her children, asleep
on the seats. Once, she had a husband, a man
who shared her trailer, who had set it, along
with a generator, among the pines at the end
of a dirt road on a mountain. Once, he cut
a winter's worth of wood, then shot a deer
and left it parceled on the table, wrapped
in butcher's paper, tied with string,
red and white, like Christmas presents.
The four hooves, positioned nearby, like a joke.
Then he hitched down the canyon
and was never seen again. So, goes her story.

Hair shot with gray rising in the static
of heated sheets ... braless, sockless, she
carried on about wingnuts, dreadlocks, drugs,
and organic flours, always smiling beatifically,
crooning a language of sacred menstruation
and coal-smoke—turning to howl then
at a stunned teenager about his cigarettes
and the violent aura she feels him conjuring
toward all creatures of the earth.

# Coming Back
### Kerri Mitchell

*Kerri Mitchell is an English faculty member at Front Range Community College. She lives in Fort Collins with her husband, Todd, ten miles east of the Poudre River. In her essay "Coming Back," she reflects on how her experience as a whitewater kayaker has taught her to cope with everyday fears.*

In May, when the snowmelt begins to release from the Rocky Mountains, my kayaker friends rub their hands together and a glint forms in their eyes. While they grin and share hopes for a high water season, I hide the erratic flutter of my heart and my nervous, shaking hands.

I've been kayaking for five years. At first I had wayward motivations for picking up the sport. I hoped to impress my husband, Todd. At the time he was only my boyfriend, and I wanted him to think I was a real bad-ass girl. So I took up the sport, unquestioningly strapping my body into a long, slender boat and shoving off into chilling, fast-moving water.

Now that I've been married for over two years, I'm far less compelled to put my life at risk for the sake of getting a guy. So what draws me back to this river each spring with my dainty blue boat tied to the roof of my car?

Every year I swear will be my last. *I'm getting too old for this,* I say. *I want to experience a long happy life, kids, old age.* But when spring hits, there I am standing on the side of the Poudre River, pulling the dry-top over my head, fastening my helmet tightly beneath my chin, and checking to see that I have my whistle (as if a whistle could save my life when I'm pinned to a rock and drowning).

Today, I'm putting my boat in on a class III–IV run named Bridges. It's a fairly popular section of the river, considered challenging at high water, but often run by moderately experienced paddlers. Today is a high-river day. I sit along the banks, strapped into my kayak, and wait for the right time to push off. Todd is playing on a wave nearby. I watch his boat gracefully surf along the foaming white pillow. He is Superman flying through clouds. I am one of Freddy Krueger's victims, running and screaming through a dark ally. My heart beats wildly and my stomach clenches. But I don't back down. I pray to the river gods, to my own God, and to any supernatural force that will listen: *Please know that I respect you deeply and honor this opportunity to paddle your waters. I beg you, don't let me die.*

I push off the shore and take my first stroke. The water feels good at first. It dances around my paddle and splashes gently against my boat. It's like a wave pool, or the log ride I used to go on at amusement parks as a kid. Even at high water, the beginning section of Bridges is always playful and smooth.

Todd and I eddy out beside a large rock on river right, and we spend a few minutes playing in the shifting currents. He throws his bow into an eddy line and I watch him launch a series of cartwheels, turning end over end. Then I follow him into the line. I lean back and spin into a little pirouette. I'm trying to convince myself that I want to be here. I'm trying to have some fun.

"You look pale and unhappy," Todd says.

"I am pale and unhappy."

"You don't have to do this."

"I know," I say. But deep down I'm sure that I do.

We paddle away from the eddy and head down the river. The rocks that normally scrape against the bottom of my boat are covered and the water flows faster than usual. So I plan my descent carefully. While Todd is scanning the river for big exciting waves to play on, I'm looking for boulders to hide behind—little pockets of refuge. I'm thinking: *What if an enormous wave flips my kayak and sucks me down into a dark hole? What if the water traps me there for hours, tossing me about like a dishrag in the wash? What if it takes them a week to get my body out?*

Todd points to a family of ducks trekking along the bank. But right now I don't care about ducks. I'm clenching my paddle, stiff and scared and mentally unfit for the challenge ahead.

Midway down the river is "Killer Bridge." It was given this name because of its nasty tendency to pin boaters to one of its pylons, flip them, and kill them. And while I've paddled this section of the river at least fifty times before, occasionally at higher water than this, I'm terrified. My limbs are shaking, clearly boycotting what I'm about to do. *We will not save you from this,* they say. *If you take us down this path we will most definitely rebel by clenching up and refusing to move until it's over.*

I respect what my shaking body is telling me. "I can't do this."

"But you've done it many times before."

"Yes, but I can't do it now. Not today."

Todd eyes the bank on river right where I'm hoping to get out. "So you're going to scale up the side of that bank?"

"Yes."

"In flip-flops?"

"Yes."

"And walk through all that poison ivy?"

"Yes."

I ferry across the river and pull my boat to the shore. When I reach the top of the bank, I begin to walk down Highway 14 making sure to position my boat on my right shoulder so that the bow will cover my face. I don't want anyone driving by to see me on my walk of shame, especially not any boaters I know. If I could, I'd hang a sign around my neck that reads: *I'm not really a wimp. I've actually paddled this section countless times. Today I just wanted to try something new, like dragging my boat through a mass of poison ivy and hiking along the shoulder of a dangerous highway.*

As I walk, I peer down at the river. It pours over enormous rocks and forms huge standing waves. From up here, this section looks manageable, so I pick my line and paddle down it in my mind. It's easy, and I make all the right moves. It's always easy when you're standing on the bank, feet firmly planted on the ground.

All my life I've been an anxious person, full of irrational fears. But over the past few years, it's gotten much worse. Some days, my fear so overwhelms me, that a regular day of work becomes a frightening descent down a class V rapid. Ten minutes before my classes begin, the "what ifs" start to creep in. *What if I don't know what I'm doing? What if I'm not really an English teacher, just a clever swindler in disguise? What if my students figure this out? What if I say something totally inappropriate or tuck my skirt into my pantyhose?* The "what ifs" pick away at my mind. They leave me feeling crazy and short of breath. They make me clench and shiver. When this happens, I reach into my backpack and pull out an index card. It reads: *I can tolerate a little anxiety knowing it will pass.* I repeat this phrase over and over. Then, I pull out another card. This one reads: *Setbacks are a part of the process and a good learning experience.* I don't actually believe this, but I say it anyway. Finally, I look at one more card, which contains a quote by Lee Upton: *Our risk is our cure.* And I believe this—wholeheartedly.

In life, as with kayaking, I'm tempted to avoid taking risks. I often think: *How can I carve out a perfectly peaceful existence where I don't have to do anything dangerous or potentially embarrassing?* The answer is: I can't. I've tried. I've attempted to hide from my fear by staying at home and taking to the couch for days at a time. But the fear comes anyway. It shows up in unlikely places. A couple of years ago, I became so cornered by my fears that I could barely order a pizza over the phone without having a panic attack.

So I have to keep going. I have to get back into the river, even when I think it will kill me.

When I reach the far side of the bridge, Todd is waiting for me. He looks up from the bank of the river, and I look down from the side of the road, and we are thinking the exact same thing: *How do I plan to get down this steep bank?*

I throw my paddle to him, so that I'll only have to carry my boat. Then I start to inch my way down. *But what if I'm toppled by the weight of my kayak? What if I trip on my tangled flip-flop and hit my head on a rock and unconsciously slide down the bank and slip into the river? Damn flip-flop.* I grab onto a tree branch and kick the flimsy sandals off. Twigs and stones poke my feet as I continue down the bank. When I'm close to the bottom, Todd reaches out and lowers my kayak to the edge of the river.

I sit for a moment and look back at Killer Bridge. The river pours smoothly around the pylons. "How was it?" I ask.

"Piece of cake. You would have had no problem. It was a whole lot easier than carrying your kayak a half-mile along a busy road."

Just then a boat full of rafters shoots out from beneath the bridge.

It looks like a family, smiling and waving at us. The youngest is about ten years old. This doesn't make me feel better.

"Are you disappointed?" I ask.

"Actually, I'm impressed. All that panic and you're still getting back in."

He's right. I don't need to feel defeated. "Our risk is our cure," I say.

Todd paddles over to give me a kiss, and with that we shove off.

As we continue through each successive rapid, my nervousness begins to subside. Each stroke gives me strength and I'm learning to take control.

When we come to a wide place in the river, I rest my paddle on the hull of my boat. I smile and wave at Todd. He winks back.

Beneath my boat, water moves along, clear and vibrant. I grab my paddle, lean to the side and tip over into the river. Then, I drift along upside down, just to feel the cold water wash over me. When I'm out of breath, I brace against my paddle, snap my hips and roll to the surface. I take a deep breath and gaze around. Dark green pine trees cover the hill sides. The canyon walls reach up toward a bright, cloudless sky. And I'm back.

# Snapping Turtle

## Jack Martin

*Jack Martin was a professional river guide for fifteen years, and he has rafted many of the rivers in the Rocky Mountain West. His poems have appeared in* Ploughshares, Black Warrior Review, The Journal, *and other magazines. His inspiration for "Snapping Turtle" (first published in* The Literary Review) *was a bike ride along the Poudre with his wife. Together they watched a big, old turtle cross the bike path and walk, stumble, and roll down a steep embankment into the river.*

I guess God must believe in me. Otherwise how would I breathe? The snapping turtle, the thirty-pound snapping turtle crawls across the black bicycle path, her legs like oars or battering rams. Her legs, each foot like four knives, her green plod across the hot pavement, and her tumble down the embankment over the concrete, the industrial scree that holds the Poudre River on her course. Her roll down the path, swimming in the gravel and chunks of concrete until she falls finally into the tear of the cold river water and swims, thick beak above the water. She beats herself against the shore and swims, tries to dig back out of the water until finally after long minutes, perhaps half an hour, she quits paddling and lets the current carry her downstream to gentler places. How could there not be a God? I find him welling in my love for my wife who stands beside me straddling her bicycle, watching. I find her welling in my wife's love for me. She is gentle and sometimes wears her hair in bangs.

# On the Trail of the Sublime Along the Poudre

Bill Tremblay

*Bill Tremblay has published seven books of poems, among them* Crying in the Cheap Seats, Duhame: Ideas of Order in Little Canada, *and* Shooting Script: Door of Fire, *which won the Colorado Book Award. A lover of the Poudre since coming to Fort Collins in 1973, he was inspired to write a novel,* The June Rise, *about the river and its history. Since becoming a member of the Poudre Wilderness Volunteers, the topic of this essay, he has been able to glut his appetite for adventures in Poudre Canyon, serving as a member of the trail crew and a mentor to new members in Leave No Trace values and practices.*

A t first, going up to the Big South was a stretch for me. It's nearly fifty miles from Ted's Place among the upper Poudre Canyon trails and includes the Arapaho-Roosevelt National Forest and the Comanche Peak Wilderness. I hiked there up to the rip-rap walkway above the dashing whitewater, a little one-mile hike on a nice day, where I stopped for lunch, watching the Cache la Poudre's headwaters, designated a "wild and scenic river area," cutting their way through the mountains.

My guidebook said the stone pavement was built by the Civilian Conservation Corps (CCC) in the 1930s. Who were they, those men? What were their lives like? What were they like? I imagined them cracking rock with eight-pound sledge hammers like a chain gang, only they were guilty of no crime except being unemployed during the Great Depression.

I wondered about that long tongue of cracked and fitted granite cobblestone. It impressed me as being powerful; it excited my imagination as a gateway to some exotic Shangri-La or Machu Picchu. Maybe it was the combination of the river's roar, the winds hollowing through the ponderosas, its lying at the base of granite cliffs, the mother of a hillside of talus that seemed—though still—to embody the motion of its slow gravitational fall.

On one trip, I brought Longinus's *On the Sublime*, which he says entails a mystery, a confrontation with place that strikes a sense of what is "beyond the human" and reduces us to silent awe. I couldn't help it; I'm a literary guy. I was teaching Wordsworth at the time, and the poet's words seemed to chime in: "The form must be of that character that deeply impresses the sense of power. And power produces the sublime."

The "sublime" is an ancient concept revived during the era of Romantic poetry. It has been roundly and often rightly parodied as ridiculously sentimental and hyped-up to the point of self-delusional, traits I admit to being guilty of on occasion. It was the belief that I could balance this infatuation with the mysterious power of nature with a strong infusion of practical knowledge that led me to join the Poudre Wilderness Volunteers. I'd gone into "transitional retirement," hoping to do some good by clearing trails while I tried to figure out what I was going to do to keep from turning into a big turnip when the semesters of teaching and nurturing the young were over.

The first time I went out with the trail crew, I drove up Highway 14 hearing once again the annual snowmelt runoff bursting over river rocks near its high-water marks in red paint past the Hanson Diversion gates. When I arrived at the campground I saw six grizzled men on the second day of a four-day mission on the upper end of Poudre Canyon— Fred, a USFS seasonal ranger, and Garin, John, and three other guys who were going up Roaring Fork. We were to hump down the whole distance of the Big South, carrying axes, six-foot crosscut saws, and tools, clearing fallen trees, ponderosas mostly, and come at it from the northwestern end upriver.

The ranger piled us in his green six-pack pickup that was geared like a Bradley Fighting Vehicle and headed off for Peterson Lake where we'd start our trek to that day's work. Finally there was no road, just a couple of old creases through the tall grass and lodgepole pine, cavernous wheel-ruts salted with boulders big enough to bang our heads on the under-roof of the cab. So we put our hard hats on just to keep our-selves from getting knocked silly.

The ranger spit his chew into a tin cup as he talked: "We lost two bull moose last week. They fought each other up on the Laramie River drainage. Punched so many holes in each other they both bled to death."

Hump! We were bounced to the roof; he spat in his chew-cup. Everybody was laughing at the ridiculous circumstances we were in as we were being made to think of the dead moose.

The pickup lurched to a stop. From there we unloaded our packs and tools. Fred gave us the "safety talk" about how to carry the tools, how to space ourselves along the trail, and how the crosscuts should be last in the line of march. We hiked through bramble and sloughs of mud inlaid with downed logs.

After a quarter of a mile or so we arrived at a point where once there had been a bridge. The concrete abutments were still there on each bank of the river. We stopped on the west bank, took our socks off and put our boots back on, slung our tools over our shoulders, and started across, fording the river where the runoff was hard, swift, and cold. I used the Combi-tool to steady myself in the flow. This far up the Big South the river seemed even stronger and wider than the Poudre down-stream.

Garin figured they must've opened the sluice gates at Peterson.

"Is that where the river begins?" I asked him.

"It begins up in Rocky Mountain National Park, but the water in Peterson is a big part of it."

I was drenched up to my belt and wearing blue jeans. By the end of that day I'd promised myself to stop being such a greenhorn and wear some fast-drying pants next time, if there were a next time, because I thought my thighs would never heal.

We arrived at a point where the stream from RMNP flows into the Big South, and it was there that we faced a deadfall maybe 36 inches in girth laid across the trail. It took some figuring before we could start.

"We'll make cuts on a bias," Garin said, holding his hands flanged out. I imagined a trapezoid. "That way, when we've cut through the barrel of the tree from two cuts, the chunk will just roll out and down the trail to the river. You don't want it dropping on your feet." So John and Garin and I set to sawing on it with our crosscut, spelling each other.

The whole thing about such work is rhythm, I quickly learned. You pull, you don't push, and you let the saw tooth blade do the work. We sawed and sawed and spelled one another until we dripped with sweat and our boots were covered with sawdust.

I had wanted this: something to do with getting to where your gear was important because you had to face the elements. Nylon pants. Boots with steel toes. Silly, I know, but as a writer sometimes it's possible to get so swallowed up in the swirling galaxies of words, and the ideas they stand for, that your psyche gets unhinged from the everyday referential world.

I hold with Wallace Stevens that poetry comes out of the tension between the imagination and what he calls "the pressures of reality," the figurative and the literal. It's not a dilemma that has to be resolved, but rather a dynamic like how the sublime is both in us and in the world. How to honor both? Is it possible to get back to where a tree is a tree and a river is a river? What's in a merely referential word? If that's all there is, where is the place for "the beyond" to happen? Yet those intuitions need grounding.

There were lots of words, or new appreciations of words. Every once in a while along the trail we'd see a big piece of bark chunked out of the side of a tree. It was a "blaze." And that was the word behind the word "trailblazer," i.e., someone who actually made a trail out of raw wilderness and marked it. I had been living in a world where the word "trailblazer" was without actual reference, except to a concept, except to another word. Or an NBA basketball team. And phrases, "widow-maker," a deadfall tree hung up in the branches of other trees that in a high wind or some other changing condition could come crashing down on the head of some unsuspecting husband. You had to stay alert, look around, which brought to mind another word, "circumspect." I liked the whole thing, the going back and forth between the popcorn sleet—a metaphor itself, that began to drum a tattoo on our hard hats—and the words for those things, especially if the things were events.

There's a passage in William Faulkner's "The Bear," where Ike McCaslin's father reads him a few lines from Keats's "Ode on a Grecian Urn" that has always haunted me. It goes like this:

> *"All right," he said. "Listen," and read again, but only one stanza this time and closed the book and laid it on the table. "She cannot fade, though thou hast not thy bliss," McCaslin said: "Forever will thou love, and she be fair."*
>
> *"He's talking about a girl," he* [the boy] *said.*
>
> *"He had to talk about some thing," McCaslin said. Then he said, "He was talking about truth. Truth is one. It doesn't change. It covers all things which touch the heart—honor and pride and pity and justice and courage and love. Do you see now?"*

Honor and pride and pity and justice and courage and love. And sublimity. And who knew when those passionate ideas were going to knock on my hard hat like popcorn sleet to remind me that in a world of dishonor and disgrace and pitilessness and injustice and cowardice and hate there must be something to gain a balance by, so that at least some of our thoughts are about something other than our problems.

The thing I learned about the Poudre right when my family and I moved out here was that it is real and can kill as well as bring life and make life possible. Cynthia and our three boys, Bill, Ben, and Jack, went up Poudre Canyon many times to camp and hike. We did the usual things: lit campfires inside the iron fire-rings and roasted marshmallows and told stories to the horizon of the river's purling rhythm in the evenings. In the mornings, we hiked up into the hills and learned the words, "angel-wing cactus," "yucca," and "rose quartz."

We often hiked the Greyrock Trail, and it was there that we first read the story on a stone monument of a boy named Vigil who'd been lost there. He haunted me, not only because his was a cautionary tale that kept reminding to watch over my sons, but also for some internal reason I could not at first fathom.

One theory was that he'd been taken by a mountain lion. I identified. I'd sit there at the summit sharing stories with my family, yet with part of me trying to imagine the boy. A poem came to me, "The Lost Boy."

Not a particularly original idea—that we are all harboring some lost child inside. Though if we can entertain the idea that the sublime happens between the rivers and us, then we can stretch a little to consider that we can make an old idea our own by expending imaginative energy on it, making it new as we make it grow. Imaginative identification is one gateway to empathy and the Infinite. That's what Blake promises us anyway.

I present the poem here to draw attention to the ending, which is another use for the sublime, that is, to imagine where we ultimately go:

**The Lost Boy**
Across the Poudre river bridge
stands a stone monument to a lost boy.
Carved words fix the mystery. Did
he wander off or was he carried off
by tooth or talon? Family, friends
searched the mountainside calling his
name. The weather turned. Sleet, wind,
snow in slants across the ponderosas.
He blacked out under the canyon's
Milky Way. I hear his cries in
echoing arroyos. Though his bones
moldered in cold drizzle he comes
crashing through wild plum thickets
clutching at my shirt, asking where I was
in his sagebrush hours. Through his
ripped jacket a flash of bone. He's forgotten
how to be alive. The climb is no relief,
his weight dogs my knees. Breezes
sough through purple yarrow, aspen groves,
dry waterfalls. I reach the cloud meadows,
hairpin switchbacks until Mount
Greyrock juts its granite forehead into
one hard thought: what remains unfinished
in the soul keeps doubling back
until earth and sky are balanced aches
like the cliff swallow's swift flight.

Here I was, drawn back into the upper Poudre Canyon, working in the rain and sleet with big hand tools, sweating and somehow better able to imagine the men from the Civilian Conservation Corps, happy to have a job, though they may have been a thousand miles from their loved ones in whatever rust-belt city they haled from and where they mailed their checks to.

The wind that blew the slanting sleet into my face sounded like the thin ghosts of those denimed workers long ago. The chill was haunting. And I felt the Poudre and the Big South that plays into it touched my heart with its truth, not only for its own beautiful sake but for the sake of those footnotes in the tumbled deadfall we call history.

By the end of the day, after a half-dozen sessions with the crosscut saw and visits to campsites and un-building fire-rings by throwing the stones in the juniper bushes, I told Garin, "This is the hardest I've worked since two-a-days." I was thinking football because John is big enough to be an NFL lineman. I asked John, "You play ball?"

"Naw. I'm not mean enough," he said.

You got to like a man like that.

There were kayakers in the Big South. I thought they must be crazy, the river was so wild that day. Two of them beached in a cove where the water rippled. They had just paddled their way through a rat's nest of logs, and they got out and took their helmets off and kneeled at the edge of the river as if they had just squirmed out of the clutches of Señor Muertos himself.

One of them said, "You were my poetry professor."

I smiled and shook his hand, and said, "I guess I'm always going to be someone's old professor."

Amid all the loud debate these days between "faith-based" versus "reality-based" thinking, what crystallized as I breathed the mist-freighted air beside the river is that I am an "imagination-based" person, something alike and something different from the squabbling voices on the radio.

Maybe writing a story about one of those Civilian Conservation Corpsmen would be a way for me to discover what was real and true for him and for his wife and kids back home in Kansas City. Maybe I could revive a story about a powerful man who grew sick and tired of the ridiculous intrigues and machinations of the halls of power and went anonymous among the ranks of the CCC to feel again the pulse of life.

The sun didn't come out that late afternoon on cue like an epiphany, and the word "sublimity" was conspicuously absent that day along the Big South. Exhausted as I was from clearing trail in rain and sleet, as I stood on the banks of the Poudre, it was cold and wet and hard on the body, yet the sublime, the Wordsworth thing, was abundant. And what is the sublime after all but the potential flood in the river that makes it awesome and beautiful and takes us out of our problems and into a meeting with the beyond?

# Cache la Poudre

James Galvin

*James Galvin was raised in northern Colorado. He has published sev-
eral collections of poetry, most recently,* Resurrection Update:
Collected Poems, 1975–1997, *in which the poem below also
appeared. He is the author of the critically acclaimed prose book,* The
Meadow, *and a novel,* Fencing the Sky. *James lives in Laramie,
Wyoming, where he has worked as a rancher part of each year all his
life, and in Iowa City, where he is a faculty member of the University
of Iowa's Writers' Workshop.*


The whole world
(Which you said I was
To you)
Thought it might lie down a minute
To think about its rivers.
It puts the case to you,
Admitting nothing,
The way rapids speculate
On the topic of stones.

The farmers on the Poudre should have known
From snuff-tin rings worn into their pockets:
Matter is a river
That flows through objects;
The world is a current
For carrying death away.
Their wooden fenceposts rotted fast in the bog
So they quarried stone posts from nearby bluffs.
You can guess what they looked like;

The worst of it was
They meant it.
Rivers neither marry,
Nor are they given in marriage;
The body floats
Face down in the soul;
The world turns over.

Those gritstone fences sank out of sight
Like a snowshoe thrown in the river.
The whole world
(Of human probability)
Lay under that hawk we found,
Face down, wings spread,
Not so much
Flying into it,
As seizing its double in the snow.

# Appendix

## Organizations Working to Preserve the Cache la Poudre River

Friends of the Poudre
www.friendsofthepoudre.org

Sierra Club: Poudre Canyon Group
www.rockymtn.sierraclub.org/pcg

Poudre Paddlers
www.poudrepaddlers.org

Trout Unlimited: Fort Collins Group
www.rockymtnflycasters.com

Citizen Planners: Fort Collins
www.fortnet.org/cp

Audubon Society: Fort Collins Chapter
www.fortnet.org/Audubon

Colorado Environmental Coalition
www.ourcolorado.org

Wolverine Farm Publishing
www.wolverinefarmpublishing.org

Colorado Water Trust
www.coloradowatertrust.org

For more information, please visit:
www.savethepoudre.org or Pulseoftheriver.org

ROCKY MOUNTAIN LAND LIBRARY

The Rocky Mountain Land Library's mission is to encourage a greater awareness of the land. Its 15,000-volume natural history library is especially focused on the land and communities of the Rocky Mountains. The subject range of this collection is both broad and deep, with hundreds of natural history studies of flora and fauna, and many more titles on ecology, conservation, astronomy, geology, paleontology, literature, poetry, Native American studies, and western regional history. Many titles address western land issues, while others concern the various cultures, both ancient and modern, that have inhabited the region.

The Land Library is currently engaged in a site search to provide both the shelves and proper environment for a unique residential land-study center for the southern Rockies. While the search continues, it is also involved in several outreach programs: the Rocky Mountain Land Series at Denver's Tattered Cover Book Store, Conversations on the Land at Colorado State University, Authors & Naturalists in the Classroom at various schools along the Front Range, the Salida Residency Program (a two-week land-study fellowship in Salida, Colorado), and a new publishing program focused on land and community in the American West.

The Rocky Mountain Land Library exists to extend everyone's knowledge of the land—waking us to the sheer miracle of life on earth, while providing access to the stewardship tools we all need. The Land Library's resources and programs are designed to meet the needs of local residents as well as far-flung visitors (naturalists, researchers, writers, and artists, among others).

For more information on the Rocky Mountain Land Library, please visit its website at www.landlibrary.org.